Survival Kit
for
Overseas Living

Survival Kit for Overseas Living

For Americans planning to live and work abroad

THIRD EDITION

L. Robert Kohls
With an Introduction by David S. Hoopes

INTERCULTURAL PRESS, INC.

For information contact
Intercultural Press, Inc.
P.O. Box 700
Yarmouth, Maine 04096 USA
207-846-5168

Book design and production by Patty J. Topel
Cover illustration and design by Tom Brown

Printed in the United States of America

00 99 98 97   4 5

Library of Congress Cataloging-in-Publication Data

Kohls, L. Robert
   Survival kit for overseas living: for Americans planning to live and work abroad / L. Robert Kohls; with an introduction by David S. Hoopes.—3rd ed.
      p. cm.
   Includes bibliographical references.
   ISBN 1-877864-38-2
   1. Americans—Foreign countries—Handbooks, manuals, etc. 2. Intercultural communication. I. Title.
E184.2.K64   1996
303.4'8273—dc20   95-23752
                                                         CIP

To Norma, my lifelong partner in the exploration
and mastery of strange lands and alien ways.

Table of Contents

Preface

I had not read *Survival Kit for Overseas Living,* originally published in 1979, since the last time I revised it (1984). To my surprise, I felt it had stood the test of time rather well and, in all humility, I felt that perhaps it might even stand up to the high praise which some in the intercultural field have given it by calling it a "classic." I have also been encouraged by the fact that, to my knowledge at least, none of my professional colleagues have criticized the fundamental premises on which the book is based. It is often easy to criticize when someone tries to simplify any body of professional knowledge so that the layperson can understand its basic concepts and apply them in practice, as in this case to living in another country.

These facts, plus the additional fact that *Survival Kit* remains the best-seller in the Intercultural Press's stable of publications, have encouraged me to bring the book up to date once again. I am most appreciative of the many people who have told me over the past decade and a half how useful this small book was in helping them personally make their adjustment to another country and its unfamiliar value system. That, after all, rather than the compliments of one's professional peers, is the real test of *Survival Kit for Overseas Living.*

Although the target readership of this book was and is the neophyte American about to experience a first extended period living abroad, it has also been a pleasant surprise to me to discover that *Survival Kit* has become one of the indispensable reference books of professional interculturalists and that it is even often adopted as a textbook in university courses in intercultural communication.

Since this is true, I would like to address a word or two in this preface to my professional colleagues.

Although as Buckminster Fuller pointed out, Spaceship Earth came without an Operator's Manual, the initial plan, when the world was sparsely populated, seems to have been that the various human groups still had enough room to allow each group to live in "its own" territory, securely separated from one another. They could live out their entire lives in comfortable isolation, relating only to members of their own family and their own clan. They had no need to communicate with neighboring strangers, much less with people from halfway around the globe.

Then the Ages of Exploration and of Colonization began to change all of that, as the Western nation-states set out to find resource-rich countries they could take and "own"—by right of their superior firepower.

Today, the impetus for contact is somewhat different, as are the means by which it occurs. We are able to travel rapidly to and communicate immediately with the far corners of the earth. The many advances in communications and transportation have meant that even the remotest parts of the world have been brought into instantaneous contact with one another. Jules Verne's 80 days have become 80 hours, 80 minutes, or even the 80 seconds or less that it takes for e-mail to span the continents.

We all tend to see these changes as advancements (if not as evolution), but at the same time, they have produced greater complexity in our lives, and they have shifted the world (while we haven't been watching) into a new paradigm. The changes they have brought about are at least as significant as those which moved human beings from the Old Stone Age into the New Stone Age, when previously nomadic bands of hunters stopped pursuing large game and began to settle down, plant and raise grains, domesticate animals, make pottery, weave cloth, and develop their settled communities.

The current shift is, if anything, even more dynamic, for it means that instead of each group living in safe and intentional isolation from each other (with their major contacts coming through trade for essential items or through warfare), suddenly, and without much preparation, the plan has changed. We are supposed to know how to live together in harmony and with respect for every other group everywhere in the world.

The old habits which were developed over centuries and which provided protection and security have suddenly become dysfunctional. Yet they are not easy to shake for, fundamentally, this paradigm shift means that while it was natural in the past to develop a preference for similarity as we related to people who were so like ourselves, it has now become more natural to experience variety and difference in our daily lives. And those who do have a preference for variety, difference, and a large range of choice in their lives seem to have a huge advantage in adapting to the constantly changing world. It is obvious that we need to develop new skills, different ones from those which our culture provided us while we were growing up. The skills that served our parents and our grandparents so well no longer serve us in the same way. The world can no longer afford the luxury of a separate space for every distinct ethnic group to have its own turf. In the United States, just within our own lifetimes, we have witnessed a striking evolution toward a multiethnic or multicultural society. We have watched as the possibilities of contact and interaction with the great variety of peoples who inhabit the world have expanded in exciting ways. We have even come to realize that our homeland is an even more special place, because it provides the world with one of the largest experiments ever witnessed in bringing together in one place and on such a grand scale peoples from all over the world. It is an exciting, hopeful experiment, made all the more difficult because there are no models to emulate. We have had to write our own Operator's Manual.

It is not easy for people to make this kind of dramatic mind-change—especially as we become more and more aware that the groups inhabiting the earth are in increasingly fierce competition for the earth's limited resources.

As an interculturalist, it is my sincere hope that we will accept this latest challenge with a spirit of goodwill toward all peoples who inhabit this planet. We will need all the compassion we can muster and a large dose of humility to meet this, the most important challenge in our history. Those who have found effective ways to express concern for others and work across cultural barriers must lead others in this essential task. We have embarked on a revolution of sorts, where building community at every level of human existence must become our overriding goal. This will require new ways of perceiving the human condition and the development of institutions which will allow humanity to thrive.

Every book is written by many people, and this one is no exception. While they do not share the title page, their imprint appears stamped clearly everywhere in the book. Without them it would never have been produced.

Revisiting one's creation of a decade and a half earlier stirs up fond memories of human contacts that span three revisions of this book. It is obvious to me that the loving contributions from coworkers in the field have left their indelible mark on the work. David S. Hoopes's suggestions were responsible for the inclusion of whole chapters in the original version (9 through 12 and 15 through 17, for example, were his idea to include). When I decided, in the second edition, to add a chapter on returning home and encountering reverse culture shock (Postscript 1), I asked Fanchon Silberstein to draft that chapter for me, and she did such a fine job of imitating my "*Time* magazine style" that there was little rewriting left for me to do. Similarly, in this third edition I asked my colleague at Global Vision Group, Claude Schnier, to conceptualize the contents of "Jaunts and Junkets" (Postscript 2), so most of the ideas in that portion of the book are his rather than mine.

Conversations with Danielle Rome Walker in 1979 were responsible for inspiring me to sit down and write the book in the first place. Serge Ogranovitch, Thomas Walker, and Jack Cook supported those early efforts. David Hoopes, Peggy Pusch, George Renwick, and Alex Patico critiqued the first edition, and all of them made valuable suggestions which greatly affected the content of the book. David and Kay Hoopes, Peggy Pusch, and Toby Frank went over this third edition with a fine-tooth comb and were an inspiration through the laborious process of rewriting it. Most authors I know argue a great deal with their editors and often look upon them as enemies, but I have always been grateful to mine for making the behind-the-scene improvements for which I will ultimately receive all the credit. They are the true unsung heroes of any publication.

L. Robert Kohls
San Francisco, 1995

Introduction

I am very pleased to have been associated with the production of this book. For years, specialists in the cross-cultural field have bemoaned the fact that a book like this did not exist. Yet none did anything about it. I often wondered why, until I got hold of Bob Kohls's manuscript. It then became clear that none of us had been able to overcome the jargon of our profession or break out of the prison of our academic training. No one was able to write a book that was substantive in content, yet couched in the language of the layperson.

Bob Kohls has done it.

Kohls has been in international and intercultural training for a long time. He's had experience in business, education, and government. As Director of Training and Development for the United States Information Agency, his daily job was to convince his colleagues that there was more to be known about functioning abroad than they thought. Later, at the Washington International Center, he had the chance to apply his ideas to orientation programs for foreign students and visitors in the United

States. Since then he has had a chance to apply his ideas in academia where, in addition to teaching beginning and advanced courses in intercultural communication, he also teaches international relations and international business courses at several universities. His workshops in intercultural awareness have been presented to mid- and upper-level managers in more than 60 of America's Fortune 500 companies.

There's an air of the author's knowing what he's about in this book. He has a flair for capturing the right idea in the right language, for making the critical points stand out, for taking you step-by-step into the intriguing heart of a sometimes baffling, sometimes frustrating, but almost always immensely rewarding experience.

But he doesn't do it ploddingly, exhausting the reader and the subject in the process. Instead, he moves you through the book at high speed, stopping to ask you questions and get you to probe your own thoughts and feelings, then taking you on at a lively pace to examine each successive stage of the overseas experience. Especially effective and valuable is Kohls's ability to keep the reader focused on the practical. He doesn't dwell on the ideas—though he makes clear the cross-cultural conceptual framework he is using. Instead, he concentrates on the practical knowledge and skills the overseas sojourner needs to "survive" in a strange land.

Given its pace and substance, this is a book you will get through quickly, but one you will think about for a long, long time.

David S. Hoopes
Intercultural Press

1

So You're Going Overseas

It's been decided. You're going to accept the opportunity to spend some time working and living in another country. Now you're getting ready, doing the thousand and one things necessary to get yourself, and perhaps your family, launched. Or maybe you're already on the plane, seat back, legs stretched out, finally able to relax for a moment and let your mind wander.

You've probably had too little time to think seriously about what's ahead, what it's going to be like living in a "foreign" country. There are few sources of good information about overseas living, and the perspective of those who've gone before you is skewed by their own particular experiences and how they've perceived them.

Yet, unless you've spent a long time in a foreign country already, there are unanticipated surprises in store. The success rate of overseas adjustment among Americans is not nearly so high as it might be. If left to luck, your chances of having a really satisfying experience living abroad would be about one in seven.

But it doesn't have to be left to luck. There are things you can do. Specifically, you and your family can give some organized thought to *planning* and *preparing* for the experience. Many people devote most of their energy to the logistics of getting launched and, in fact, *do* leave the rest to luck. The wiser person looks further ahead. There may be many unknowns or uncertainties but it's possible to lay the groundwork for a productive time overseas. The purpose of this book is to show how it can be done.

Curiously, what people need most when they go overseas is to understand themselves better as Americans—because when they go they carry with them all the "cultural baggage" they have accumulated during their lifetime. One purpose of this book is to help you become aware of *your* cultural baggage and suggest ways in which to avoid tripping over it too often. To do so we need to ask what it is in the American environment that has made you what you are and how an awareness of your *Americanness* can provide the basis for understanding and coping effectively with your experiences in a foreign country.

Over there, the environment and the culture have been busy shaping people into Germans, Japanese, Arabs, Chinese, Colombians, or whatever. The question is: How can you as an American direct your efforts toward learning, in the quickest, most cost-effective manner, how to function at your optimum capacity in the non-American environment into which you are soon to be, quite literally, dropped?

The material presented in these pages is designed to provide the answers to those questions. The ideas are stated as succinctly as possible and yet attempt to get at some of the deeper issues which are central to functioning effectively overseas.

The book doesn't preach. More often than not you will be asked to think through the issues on your own in brief, structured exercises. The book should be seen as a resource for getting you into and through an experience which, like whitewater rafting, is exciting and rewarding, but which has its shoals and rapids. It's a book you can come back to when the going gets rough. It's a *Survival Kit for Overseas Living.*

2

Others Have Gone Before

You're not the first American to leave our shores to try your hand at living in another country. Thousands have gone before and set the stage for your arrival....
Yes, your way has been paved—with bad impressions!
All over the world people think they know all about Americans. They've watched American tourists, American films, and American TV programs. Their radios and newspapers have blared forth sensational news about the United States. They've heard incredible stories from friends and relatives who have visited the United States.
The result has been, at best, an incomplete view of what Americans are like; at worst, a distorted one. Out of this incomplete or distorted information have emerged stereotypes—fixed, simplified impressions of what Americans are. Stereotypes are natural; they are one way people everywhere deal with things which are too complex to handle or about which they have inadequate information.
But they are also destructive in personal encoun-

ters because they are unfair and because they interfere with getting to know people.

You will be confronted often with stereotypes. People will judge you not on the basis of who you are and the signals you give off, but on the stereotypes they formed long before they knew you existed.

How will you respond? What kinds of stereotypes do you think you will encounter? Take a moment before turning the page to jot down in the space provided some of the stereotypes of Americans you think are most commonly held abroad.

Then go on and see how they compare with our list.

Duane Hanson sculpture, *Tourists* (1970), photographed by Eric Pollitzer.

3

The Stereotyped American

Here are some of the most common stereotypes of Americans held by people in other countries.

Americans are:

- Optimistic
- Outgoing, friendly
- Informal
- Loud, rude, boastful, immature
- Naive
- Hardworking
- Aggressive
- Judgmental, moralistic
- Superficial
- Extravagant, wasteful
- Confident they have all the answers
- Politically naive and/or uninformed
- Ignorant of other countries
- Disrespectful of authority
- Wealthy

- Materialistic
- Generous
- Impatient, always in a hurry

It is also widely believed that:

- All American women are promiscuous

How many of the listed items are positive and how many are negative? Go through and put a check beside the positive ones and underline the negative ones.

Most of us would probably consider six or seven of the points to be positive. To Americans, "outgoing, friendly" and "informal," to mention only a couple, are considered to be virtues. Yet, the reserved Britisher who finds his seatmate on a transatlantic flight an outgoing, backslapping American may have quite a different opinion. Someone from a country with a very structured, hierarchical social system, such as India, may consider our informality an affront.

The point is that what we think are positive values or admirable characteristics may not be considered so by others. What we believe to be a positive stereotype may, in fact, be a negative one in the eyes of a person from another country.

Which brings us to a fundamental point: Throughout the world there are many different ways of doing things, most of which are intrinsically neither better nor worse than our own. They are simply different.

Stereotypes are not necessarily wrong. Some of them contain too much truth for comfort. The problem with stereotypes, really, is that they prevent us from getting to the richer reality which lies beyond them.

One thing is certain: At some point when you are overseas, you will encounter these stereotypes and there will be those who will hold you *personally* responsible for them. It's very likely you will be called upon to answer some very pointed questions based on them.

When we asked you about how you would respond to being stereotyped, what were your thoughts? What will you say in reply if someone asks you: "Why are Americans such racists? Such imperialists? So rude? So rushed all the time?"

There are no pat answers, of course. Each person must form his or her own unique responses. Experience has shown, however, that the following are useful guidelines:

1. Resist becoming angry or defensive.

2. Avoid fitting negative stereotypes.

3. Persist in being your (sweet old) self.

If your sweet old self fits one of the stereotypes, then you've got a problem. Better in the beginning to avoid the stereotype and to let your real personality emerge as you become more comfortable in the environment.

Indeed, anything you can do to help break the negative stereotypes people have of Americans will contribute 1) to your own pleasure in the overseas experience, 2) to the pleasure of those who follow you, 3) to the improvement of the American image abroad, and 4) perhaps a smidgen to world understanding. Quite a collection of accomplishments for so small an effort.

Now let's look at the other side of the stereotyping coin. All over the world there are friendly, hospitable people ready and eager to welcome Americans into their societies.

What kinds of attitudes do we as a group have about them and their cultures? Are we ever guilty of a little counterproductive stereotyping of our own?

4

The Ugly American

The novel *The Ugly American*[1] struck the Americans of the late 1950s like a thunderbolt. It came at a time when the nation was moving internationally into high gear. Americans were swarming about the world as never before. Tourists, diplomats, students, scholars, technical experts, business executives, and military advisers were spreading an image of Americans which came to be embodied in many of the negative stereotypes discussed in the previous chapter. *The Ugly American* held a mirror up before us, and it was with a distinct shock that we recognized the reflection we saw. We were embarrassed by the behaviors and attitudes Americans displayed as guests in other countries.

To a significant extent because of *The Ugly American* we are much more conscious today of our be-

---

[1] By Eugene Burdick and William Lederer (New York: Norton, 1958). Ironically, the "Ugly American" in the book was in reality the good guy, who was sensitive to other cultures. The term was soon turned around, however, to refer to the loud, insensitive, exploitative brand of overseas American.

havior overseas, particularly in our words and deeds. We still carry with us, however, a number of deeply embedded attitudes which tap into our darker nature and emerge from time to time in our international contacts.

Following is a list of some of those attitudes. A number are quite commonly held and may not, at first glance, seem offensive. Others are to be found only in the extremely narrow-minded or, indeed, in the bigot. Look the list over and check those which reflect what you feel is a defensible position.

1. The fact that the United States was able to place a man on the moon proves American technological superiority.
2. Foreigners coming to live in the United States should give up their foreign ways and adapt to the United States as quickly as possible.
3. Asians do many thing backwards.
4. Much of the world's population remains underdeveloped because they don't take the initiative to develop themselves.
5. English should be accepted as the universal language of the world.
6. The Vietnamese and other Southeast Asians do not place value on human life; to them life is cheap.
7. Americans have been very generous in teaching other people how to do things the right way.
8. Minority members of a population should conform to the customs and values of the majority.
9. If everyone learned to do things the way we do them, the world would be better off and

people everywhere would understand each other better.
10. Primitive people have not yet reached the higher stages of civilization.

Can you convert these into objective statements? For instance, change item 1 to: "By placing a man on the moon, the United States demonstrated the great emphasis which it as a society places on technological development." Consider the others.

More important—as they stand, what central theme runs through all of these statements?

Look them over again carefully before reading on.

State the central theme briefly in the space below.

The theme as we see it: the implicit assumption of the superiority of one group over another, humankind's ancient ethnocentric[2] impulse. We all believe in our heart of hearts that our race, our culture, our group is the most important, worthy, civilized, etc., in the world. It's a primordial instinct which from the beginning of the species has served a basic survival function by linking us to and strengthening the group from which we derive our security, thus assuring the group's continuance.

---

[2] Webster's definition of ethnocentrism is: "Regarding one's own race or cultural group as superior to others."

Unfortunately it is also a destructive impulse from which war, hate, oppression, and prejudice flow. There is little hope of ever being wholly freed from it because it is a largely subconscious impulse and influences our attitudes and behaviors without our being aware of it.

But there are things we can do to control our ethnocentrism, and we will examine them one-by-one in the chapters which follow.

First, however, let's take a closer look at one of the attitudes which crops up all too often as a stumbling block to effectiveness overseas.

5

Primitivism Reconsidered

"Primitive people have not yet reached the higher stages of civilization."
For anyone involved in international activities, this is an especially insidious belief.
All of us, by virtue of our enculturation[1] in Western society in general, and in American society in particular, have deeply embedded within us certain ideas regarding what it means to be civilized and what it means to be primitive.
Think, for a moment, of the dictionary definition of the words "civilization" and "primitive."
We have been taught that civilization represents an advanced state of human development, with an extremely high level of achievement and sophistication in the arts and sciences, technology, government, and social institutions. (To us, even our religion has long since moved out of the morass of superstition and magic.)

---

[1] Enculturation is an anthropological term which refers to the process of being trained in the values and behaviors of one's parent society.

Primitive, on the other hand, denotes a state of simplicity bordering on ignorance, or at least on the simplicity of the untutored child. That which is primitive is rudimentary, unsophisticated, and superstitious. Primitive peoples, according to the common definition, are closer to the state of our primordial ancestors who wandered the forests on all fours looking for food and shelter.

The picture we carry in our minds looks something like this:

Civilized

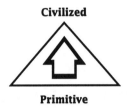

Primitive

Of course, *we're* the ones who are civilized.

This idea flowered in nineteenth-century Europe when, under the influence of Darwin, theorists attempted to apply the idea of evolution to the development of society as a whole. One of the results was that Europeans at that time saw themselves as the end product and at the apex of human civilization.

This kind of thinking was graphically epitomized by Lewis Morgan, a well-known anthropologist of the period, in his "Pyramid of Human Development."

To accompany the Pyramid, Morgan developed clear and precise definitions for each stage, from "lower savagery" to "higher civilization," and then classified every known group of people within one of the stages.

This once-respected work now seems ludicrous. It would no longer be accepted by anthropologists anywhere (that in itself is a sign we've made some advances in cultural awareness!).

Lewis Morgan's "Pyramid of Human Development"

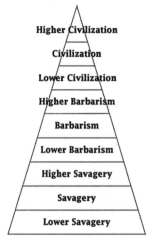

We know now that most societies once called primitive are in fact highly developed civilizations with complex and sophisticated social structures and cultural patterns, each with its own peak achievements. They have been judged too often, however, on their failure to encompass the technological and scientific accomplishments of the West.

But Morgan's basic ideas linger in our present attitudes toward non-Western peoples, even though many of us have long since learned that it is not acceptable to refer to a specific country or its people as primitive, at least not to their faces. Yet the persistent problem of how we should refer politely to the people who are so different from ourselves remains.

Ethnocentrism being what it is, throughout history peoples have tended to conceptualize the outsider as some sort of lesser being than their own kin. The Chinese, historically and traditionally, conceived of everyone outside their borders as "barbarians." So did the ancient Greeks. The Europeans, who thought it was they who discovered

19

America, considered the people they found there to be savages. A hundred years ago these words were used straightforwardly, descriptively, and without shame.

More recently, these outsiders were called uncivilized and primitive. Then, as we began to realize the insults which were inherent in those terms, it became popular to speak of them as natives or aborigines.

Just as we began to become self-conscious about how we referred to peoples of other cultures (and, especially, the concepts behind the words), we became equally uneasy about how we designated the countries in which they lived. We called them, in turn,

undeveloped countries

underdeveloped countries

less developed countries or LDCs (without saying what the letters actually stood for)

and, then, developing countries.

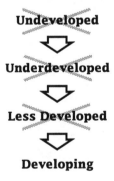

In the end, *all* these terms—even "developing"—were disparaging and demeaning, implying the inherent superiority of developed countries and carrying the seed of the idea that, of course, they would eventually aspire to becoming developed *just like us.*

The French, in 1952, first coined the term "Third World" to indicate not two but three forms of *political* alignment. The industrialized Western democracies were the "First World." The communist countries were the "Second World." And those countries which chose not to align themselves with either the First or Second Worlds were called "Third World." Gradually the term "Third World" began to take on an *economic* meaning instead of its original political meaning. In 1979, *Time* magazine was the first to point out that, economically speaking, there are actually *five* worlds.[2]

Other recent attempts to devise acceptable terms to designate peoples and nations so different from ourselves include:

Pre-literate Societies,
Pre-industrial Societies,
NICs (Newly Industrialized Countries) or NIEs (Newly Industrialized Economies), and Nonaligned Countries.

Others include:

Indigenous peoples, Non-Western Countries, Non-Western Peoples, Host Country Nationals (or just Nationals), or Traditional Societies.

"Third World Countries" or "Third World Peoples" are probably the least derogatory terms currently in use, if only because they imply that their ways

---

[2] By this expanded classification, the First and Second Worlds remained the same, while the Third World came to include countries like South Korea and Taiwan which, economically, had almost made it into the First World. The "Fourth World" became countries like Brazil and India which were still far from "developed," but which had sufficient natural resources to eventually become fully "developed," or First World. The "Fifth World" was made up of countries like Bangladesh and Chad which are so poor that there is little hope that they will become First World in the foreseeable future.

represent a conscious alternative to our own and a *legitimate* choice.

All of these terms represent honest attempts to deal with a problem that will not quietly go away: What *do* we call the people who are so different from ourselves? They also point out the embarrassing fact that the ethnocentrism that lies behind Lewis Morgan's Pyramid still lurks deep within us all.

Another thing we can do to neutralize the effect of Morgan's ideas is to compare cultures on a co-equal basis, as in the diagram below. If we call the two cultures "X culture" (instead of "civilized") and "Z culture" (instead of "primitive"), we can show them without making assumptions of superiority:

Any areas of commonly held values which exist, and there are usually many, may be diagrammed in this way:

This takes us back now to our earlier question: How do you go about bringing your ethnocentrism under control?

The answer: You bring it to the surface, look at it, and shift the emphasis from cultural inferiority and superiority to cultural similarities and differences— as we have done with our *X* and *Z* cultures.

Another useful undertaking is to become acquainted with the nature of culture itself.

6

Culture Defined

The word "culture" has literally dozens of definitions—most of which will be ignored here. By culture, for instance, we do not mean that which characterizes the intellectually and socially "cultured" person, nor do we refer to the arts—literature, painting, the opera, etc. These are valid meanings of the word, but not what is being referred to here.

Instead, we are using culture in the anthropological sense. For the purposes of this book here is the definition we like best:

> **Culture** = an integrated system of learned behavior patterns that are characteristic of the members of any given society. Culture refers to the total way of life of particular groups of people. It includes everything that a group of people thinks, says, does, and makes—its systems of attitudes and feelings. Culture is learned and transmitted from generation to generation.

By this definition, we can see that a particular culture would consist of at least the following:

- Manners
- Customs
- Beliefs
- Ceremonies
- Rituals
- Laws (written and unwritten)
- Ideas and thought patterns
- Language
- Arts and artifacts
- Tools
- Social institutions
- Religious beliefs
- Myths and legends
- Knowledge
- Values
- Concept of self
- Morals
- Ideals
- Accepted ways of behaving

In short, culture is the total way of life of any group of people.

It is obvious, therefore, that culture is woven intricately into the very fiber of every member of the group and is a controlling influence in the way people live, the way they think, the way they speak, and the way they behave. When these "patterns of culture," which are built into each of us, encounter other and different patterns of culture (as occurs when you go from your own culture group to live in another, for example), conflict, dissonance, and disorientation are the almost inevitable result.

Culture, thus, is central to the experience of living overseas. The next several chapters will be spent delving rather deeply into what culture is and how it affects you as an American.

Now that we have a working definition of culture, we're ready to make a number of generalizations which follow naturally one from the other:

1. By definition, to be human means to be part of a culture. It is impossible to conceive of humans outside of culture. Humans create culture and culture creates humans.

2. Most cultures developed separately, in isolation, thousands of years ago. The ways in which each eventually developed were adapted and evolved slowly and painstakingly, through trial and error, by each group independently. The course of this evolution was based primarily on the ability of each element in the culture to contribute to the physical and psychological survival of the group.

3. The culture of any group represents an extremely complex and interrelated package where every aspect is interwoven and enmeshed with all other aspects. To change any one part of a culture inevitably affects many other parts of the culture.

4. Every society, in developing its own culture, must meet the needs of the group in at least ten basic areas. The first three items on the following list are generally recognized as the necessities of life, especially important to the individual members of the culture. If we speak of society as a whole, however, the next seven items may be seen as equally necessary to maintain culture.

- Food
- Clothing
- Shelter
- Family organization
- Social organization
- Government
- Defense
- Arts/Crafts
- Knowledge/Science
- Religion

5. It was highly likely, indeed almost inevitable, that different groups would come up with different sets of solutions to these ten basic needs.

6. There are no intrinsically right or wrong solutions, no objectively provable better or worse ways of meeting these needs. There are no absolutes. For practical purposes, there are only *different* solutions. This is a key point and a very complex issue. We are not advocating ethical or moral neutrality. Approval of such practices as head shrinking, human sacrifice, or cannibalism is not required or even recommended in order to recognize that there is an *inherent logic* in every culture. To understand different values and behaviors, it is useful to approach them nonjudgmentally, searching for that which is inherently logical rather than automatically either condemning or accepting them.

7. An equally key point is that every group of people, every culture is, and has always been, ethnocentric; that is, it thinks its own solutions are superior and would be recognized

as superior by any right-thinking, intelligent, logical human being. It is significant that to each group, its own view of the world appears to be the "common sense" or "natural" view. Let's take a brief look at Americans and the cultural characteristic of cleanliness by way of example. We generally consider ourselves among the cleanest people in the world. We're quick to criticize many other countries and cultures as being dirty. Yet consider the following:

- When Americans bathe, they soak, wash, and rinse their bodies in the same water—though they would never wash their clothes and dishes that way. The Japanese, who use different water for each of these steps, find the American way of bathing hard to understand, even dirty.

- An orthodox Hindu from India considers it dirty to eat with knives, forks, and spoons instead of with his or her own clean fingers.

- Is it dirtier to spit and blow your nose on the street or to carry it around with you in a little piece of cloth which you keep in your pocket and reuse regularly?

- Many people around the world cannot understand why Americans invariably defecate in the same room where they wash and bathe, or why, in so many modern American homes, the toilet is placed so near the kitchen.

8. The process through which the accumulated culture of any group is passed on to its offspring is called "enculturation." Every person is enculturated into a particular culture. One

could say that each society enculturates its own offspring into its own "right way" of doing things.

9. People who stay strictly within their own cultures can go on indefinitely without ever having to confront their ethnocentric or enculturated selves.

10. Problems arise, however, when a person who is enculturated into one culture is suddenly dropped into another, very different culture.

It is at this point, as we mentioned earlier, that conflict, dissonance, and disorientation set in. The common term for this effect is "culture shock." Everyone going to live in a new environment will experience culture shock in some degree. They will also be offered the opportunity to learn and grow in unique and exciting ways.

We'll talk about culture shock in more detail later.

Right now, in order to provide you with a basis for both coping with the overseas experience and exploiting it to the fullest for your own benefit, we need to explore how best to interpret and analyze cultures. What you need are some tools—conceptual tools, in this case—which will enable you to sort out the basic elements of culture and deal with them rationally and systematically.

7

Comparing and Contrasting Cultures

The husband and wife team of Clyde and Florence Kluckhohn, along with fellow anthropologist Frederick Strodtbeck, have provided us with one of the needed tools. Looking at the phenomenon of culture analytically and philosophically, they came up with five basic questions that get at the root of any culture's value system, no matter how different or seemingly exotic.

1. What is the character of innate human nature? = Human nature orientation

2. What is the relation of humans to nature? = Relationship to nature orientation

3. What is the temporal focus (time sense) of human life? = Time orientation

4. What is the mode of human activity? = Activity orientation

5. What is the mode of human relationships? = Social orientation

Consider for a moment the five orientations in the right-hand column. How would you describe the attitude of the majority of Americans toward each? What do Americans think human beings are like basically? What kind of relationship do they have to nature? What does time mean to them? How important is action? What kind of relationship do they have with each other?

The chart which follows is an adaptation and simplification of one developed by Kluckhohn and Strodtbeck. It indicates the range of possible responses to the five orientations. It is intended to be read horizontally, each horizontal box relating to one of the five orientations listed above.[1]

ORIENTATION	BELIEFS AND BEHAVIORS		
Human Nature	Basically Evil	Mixture of Good and Evil	Basically Good
Relationship to Nature	Humans Subjugated by Nature	Humans in Harmony with Nature	Humans the Masters of Nature
Sense of Time	Past-oriented	Present-oriented	Future-oriented
Activity	Being (Stress on who you are)	Growing (Stress on self-development)	Doing (Stress on action)
Social Relationships	Authoritarian	Group-oriented	Individualistic

We recognize that in any culture consisting of a large number of people, the whole range of possible human values and behaviors will probably be found, if only in a few individuals. When we talk of American or French or Chinese values, we mean

---

[1] A full outline of the Kluckhohn Model is included in Appendix A.

those which predominate within that group, those which are held by enough of its members to make the values an evident and prominent part of the culture as a whole. Let's take a look at each of the five orientations to determine where a typical middle-class American might be expected to fit.[2]

In respect to HUMAN NATURE, average, middle-class/ mainstream Americans are generally optimistic, choosing to believe the best about a person until that person proves otherwise. Will Rogers, the American humorist, was being very American when he said: "I never met a man I didn't like." We would place the average American's beliefs about human nature in the right-hand column (basically good) as far as Human Nature Orientation goes. This classification explains the interest Americans have in such activities as prison reform and social rehabilitation. Americans generally believe that in order to bring out the basic goodness in human beings all you have to do is change the negative social conditions in which they exist.[3] Indeed, deep down, Americans in general believe humans and human society are ultimately perfectible—if only enough effort is made in that direction.

---

[2] Members of American minority groups would probably find their values diverging in some significant respects from those discussed here. If you are a member of a minority or have a strong ethnic identification, attempt to identify ways in which your values and behavior differ from those indicated here as characteristic of mainstream American culture.

[3] The Kluckhohns placed Americans in the left-hand column (basically evil), citing the Christian belief in original sin. This may have been an accurate reading for the 1950s, though we have our doubts. But whether Americans see human nature as good or evil, it is certainly fair to say they accept it as changeable.

In their relationship to NATURE, Americans see a clear separation between humans and nature (this would be incomprehensible to many Asians), and humans are clearly held to be in charge. The idea that people can control their own destiny is totally alien to most of the world's cultures. Elsewhere people tend to believe that they are driven and controlled by fate and can do very little, if anything, to influence it. Americans, on the other hand, have a strong drive to subdue, dominate, and control their natural environment.

Concerning orientation toward TIME, Americans are dominated by a belief in progress. We are future-oriented. This implies a strong task, or goal, orientation. We are very conscious too that "time is money" and therefore not to be wasted. We have an optimistic faith in the future and what the future will bring. We tend to equate "change" with "improvement" and consider a rapid rate of change as normal.

As for ACTIVITY, Americans are so action-oriented that they cannot even conceive what it would be like to be "being-oriented." Indeed, we are *hyperactive,* to the degree that one sociologist has described the American as an "Electric Englishman." We believe in keeping busy and productive at all times— even on vacation. The faith of Horatio Alger in the work ethic is very much with us. As a result of this action orientation, Americans have become very proficient at problem solving and decision making.

Our SOCIAL orientation is toward the importance of the individual and the equality of all people. Friendly, informal, outgoing, and extroverted, Americans scorn rank and authority, even when they are the ones with the rank and authority. American bosses are almost the only supervisors in the world who insist on their subordinates calling them by their first names. We find it extremely easy to make friends, and we think there are unlimited friendships out there just waiting to be made. With a strong sense of individuality, family ties in America are weak, especially when compared to the rest of the world. We have succeeded in reducing the family to its smallest possible unit—the nuclear family. Look back at the Kluckhohn-Strodtbeck Model on page 30. If we take the structure of compartments as shown there and fill in the areas into which the predominant American values fall, we come up with a picture of the American value system that looks like this:

		Basically Good (changeable)
		Humans the Masters of Nature
		Future-oriented
		Doing (Stress on action)
		Individualistic

Let's look at the value systems of several other societies and compare them with the American.

We recognize that models of this kind are oversimplifications and can only give approximations of reality. Their use is in giving rough pictures of the striking contrast and differences which may be encountered in societies where certain values predominate, even though they may be in the process of marked change due to rapid modernization. Fundamental values, however, have a way of persisting in spite of change. The evolution of values is a slow process, since they are rooted in survival needs and passed on, almost fanatically, from generation to generation.

We see many of the world's traditional cultures as follows:

Basically Evil		Mixture of Good and Evil		
	(unchangeable)		(unchangeable)	
Humans Subjugated by Nature				
Past-oriented				
Being (Stress on who you are)				
Authoritarian				

Here's how we view Arab cultures from a generalized perspective. There would be important variations, of course, from one specific culture to another—Egyptian, Saudi, Lebanese, etc. Notice that in one category (humans' relationship to the natural environment), Arabs seem to fall more or less equally into two of the classifications.

	Neutral		
		(unchangeable)	
Humans Subjugated by Nature	Humans in Harmony with Nature		
Past-oriented			
Being (Stress on who you are)			
Authoritarian			

Here's how we see the Japanese (a very complex culture and even more "contradictory" than the Arabs):

	Mixture Good/Evil		
		(unchangeable)	
	Humans in Harmony with Nature		
Past-oriented			Future-oriented
	Growing		Doing
Authoritarian	Group-oriented		

The Kluckhohn chart only shows three variations out of an infinite variety of possibilities, and it only compares culture on five basic orientations. It does not claim, therefore, to tell you *everything* about every conceivable culture. Yet it is impressive in the differences in values which it does reveal. In a sense, the values expressed in the right-hand column can be said to be 180° away from the values in the left-hand column.

Is it any wonder that putting Americans into cultures with complex and/or radically different value orientations sometimes causes stress, disorientation, and breakdowns in communication?

In a very simple format, the Kluckhohn chart indicates where the problems are likely to lie.[4] Plot

---

[4] For a study that elaborates on the Kluckhohn model and includes some interesting cross-cultural comparisons see Edward C. Stewart and Milton J. Bennett, *American Cultural Patterns: A Cross-Cultural Perspective* (Yarmouth, ME: Intercultural Press, 1991).

the culture to which you are going in comparison to a middle-class American orientation (or to your own orientation if it varies from the American norm). To do so may call for a little extra reading or a talk with someone who knows the country well.

8

What Makes an American?

The use of models, while helpful, tends to be an abstract, academic way of getting at the subject. How can we bring American values, which constitute the core piece of cultural baggage you are taking overseas with you, more sharply into focus?

Have you ever sat down and tried to make a list of American values? Or perhaps "basic ideas held by most Americans"? If you're not an anthropologist or cultural historian, it probably won't be easy. But since it's relevant, give it a try.

Write in the space which follows as many American values or basic American ideas or beliefs as you can think of. Wherever possible, condense them into one- or two-word phrases.

VALUES:

How many did you get? If you have more than ten you're satisfied with, that's good.

There's another way to get at the concrete yet evasive values which guide our lives, a way so simple and integral to the experience of growing up that you may be startled by how easy it is to open a window on what makes us tick as Americans.

In the space below jot down quickly as many proverbs, axioms, and adages as you can dredge up from your memory, sayings like: "A watched pot never boils" or "A stitch in time saves nine."

How many can you think of?

PROVERBS:

If your memory is deficient, don't worry. We'll help. But if you did get a list, go back over it before reading further and write down beside each proverb what value you think it is teaching—again in a one- or two-word phrase.

Now, here is our list—the proverbs on the left and the values they seem to be teaching on the right.

Cleanliness is next to godliness.	CLEANLINESS
A penny saved is a penny earned.	THRIFTINESS
Time is money.	TIME THRIFTINESS
Don't cry over spilt milk.	PRACTICALITY
Waste not; want not.	FRUGALITY
Early to bed, early to rise, makes a man healthy, wealthy, and wise.	DILIGENCE; WORK ETHIC
God helps those who help themselves.	INITIATIVE
It's not whether you win or lose, but how you play the game.	GOOD SPORTSMANSHIP
A man's home is his castle.	PRIVACY; VALUE OF PERSONAL PROPERTY
No rest for the wicked (weary).	GUILT, WORK ETHIC
You've made your bed, now lie in it.	RESPONSIBILITY; RETALIATION
Don't count your chickens before they hatch.	PRACTICALITY
A bird in the hand is worth two in the bush.	PRACTICALITY
The squeaky wheel gets the grease.	AGGRESSIVENESS
Might makes right.	SUPERIORITY OF PHYSICAL POWER
There's more than one way to skin a cat.	ORIGINALITY; DETERMINATION

A stitch in time saves nine.	TIMELINESS OF ACTION
All that glitters is not gold.	WARINESS
Clothes make the man.	CONCERN FOR PHYSICAL APPEARANCE
If at first you don't succeed, try, try again.	PERSISTENCE; WORK ETHIC
Take care of today and tomorrow will take care of itself.	PREPARATION FOR FUTURE
Laugh and the world laughs with you; weep and you weep alone.	POSITIVE ATTITUDE

Our proverbs list is by no means complete, but we have already enumerated 20 basic American values:

- CLEANLINESS
- THRIFTINESS
- TIME THRIFTINESS
- PRACTICALITY
- FRUGALITY
- DILIGENCE
- INITIATIVE
- GOOD SPORTSMANSHIP
- PRIVACY
- WORK ETHIC

- RESPONSIBILITY
- AGGRESSIVENESS
- PHYSICAL POWER
- ORIGINALITY
- TIMELINESS OF ACTION
- WARINESS
- PHYSICAL APPEARANCE
- PERSISTENCE
- PREPARATION FOR FUTURE
- POSITIVE ATTITUDE

It is evidently much more potent in teaching practicality, for example, to say, "Don't cry over spilt milk" than "You'd better learn to be practical." We have all heard this axiom hundreds of times, and it has made its point.

9

To See Ourselves

"Oh wad some Power the giftie gie us/To see oursels as ithers see us!" wrote Robert Burns. Robbie was inspired to this thought by a louse crawling on the bonnet of a lady in the pew in front of him in church, but down through the years we've gotten the message.

What Burns didn't know is that we have had that gift all along but haven't realized it. By lowering our defenses and viewing ourselves through the eyes of people from other cultures—from what is called the "cross-cultural perspective"—we can get a strikingly refreshing view of ourselves. But we have to be ready to accept the reality of what we see, warts (or lice) and all.

We are doomed to carry our complete load of cultural baggage wherever we go. There will be no stripping down to lighten the burden or to make the trip easier. It's important, therefore, to know as much as possible about what our culture has packed for us to carry endlessly about the world.

We believe that every culture has a rough balance between positive and negative aspects. Therefore, to point out the weaker or more negative aspects along with the positive in the process of examining a culture or value system does not constitute an attack on that culture. For me to become more aware of my cultural self in its fullest dimensions is a source of strength because it reinforces my real worth rather than an ethnocentric view of reality. To know ourselves better is to grow.

Let's look at ourselves, then, from a cross-cultural perspective. Let's listen to some opinions of Americans and American ways held by sensitive, observant, and essentially sympathetic foreign visitors.

In 1835, the Frenchman Alexis de Tocqueville visited America and on his return to France wrote a book[1] containing such astute observations about the new American Republic that many are as valid today as they were then.

Modern de Tocquevilles—from all over the world—still are intrigued by the intricacies and enigmas of American culture. Here is a selection of observations by foreign visitors to this country.[2] As you read them, take time to ask yourself in each case: 1) Is the observation accurate? and 2) How would you explain the trait in question?

---

[1] *Democracy in America* is still well worth reading. London: Saunders and Otley, 1835-1840 (four volumes).

[2] Examples one through seven and number nine are from John P. Fieg and John G. Blair, *There Is a Difference,* Washington, DC: Meridian International Center, 1975; example eight is from Anthony Scarangello, *American Education through Foreign Eyes,* New York: Dorman, 1967; number ten is from the film series *Going International,* produced by Griggs Productions, San Francisco.

Visitor from
1. India:

> ...Americans seem to be in a perpetual hurry. Just watch the way they walk down the street. They never allow themselves the leisure to enjoy life; there are too many things to do....

2. Australia:

> I am impressed by the fact that American teachers never seem to stop going to school themselves.

3. Turkey:

> Once we were out in a rural area in the middle of nowhere and saw an American come to a stop sign. Though he could see in both directions for miles and no traffic was coming, he still stopped!

4. Colombia:

> The tendency in the U.S. to think that life is only work hits you in the face. Work seems to be the one type of motivation....

5. Japan:

> Americans seem to feel like they have to say something instead of having silence—even when what they say is so well known that it sounds stupid. They say things that are so obvious. Japanese people realize that we have all observed these things so it is unnecessary to talk about them.

6. Vietnam:

> Americans are handy people. They do almost everything in the house by themselves, from painting walls and doors to putting glass in their windows. Most of them showed me the pretty tables and bookshelves they made by themselves in their spare time.

7. Iran:

> The first time...my [American] professor told me, "I don't know the answer, I will have to look it up," I was shocked. I asked myself, "Why is he teaching me?" In my country a professor would give a wrong answer rather than admit ignorance.

8. Japan:

> Unfortunately, I was given a bad impression by some American students who speak of their own country very poorly, especially of its foreign policy. I knew all the foreign policy of America was not good, but I did not want to be told so by a native. I hate people who speak badly of their own land, even if they speak the truth.

9. Colombia:

> I was surprised in the United States to find so many young people who were not living with their parents, although they were not yet married. Also, I was surprised to see so many

single people of all ages living alone, eating alone, and walking the streets alone. The United States must be the loneliest country in the world.

10. The Netherlands:

Imagine my astonishment when I went to the supermarket and looked at eggs. You know, there are no small eggs in America; they just don't exist. They tend to be jumbo, extra large, large, or medium. It doesn't matter that the medium are little. Small eggs don't exist [in America] because, I guess, they think that might be bad or denigrating.

These observations are worth examining carefully. They reveal a great deal about us as Americans. For example, take item 7:

Most American professors take their status less seriously than Iranian professors do. They prefer to cultivate informal, straightforward relationships with their students, often to the point of accepting virtual equality of status. This may go so far as viewing themselves as learners along with the students.

In Iran, where teachers are venerated, this attitude would not be encountered. Students would lose respect for teachers who behaved as American professors do.

American students, on the other hand, approve of the informal, equal-status behavior of their teachers. Americans in general tend to be somewhat skeptical of experts—though they depend heavily on them in crises. But they expect experts to cultivate an air of modesty. Those who are unafraid to admit their ignorance gain our respect. In much of the rest of the world, however, attitudes toward equality and expertise and formality and informality are quite different.

Before going on, try your hand at explaining the rest of the modern "de Tocquevillisms" listed above.

10

Traveling by Objectives

It is common in management circles these days to spend a lot of time discussing and setting objectives. Yet how often do we think about setting objectives in our personal lives?

Indeed, how carefully have you examined the motivations which have led you to opt for the overseas assignment? It might be useful to stop for a moment and examine them again. They are very important because if you are not clear as to exactly what your goals are in going abroad, you will have no way of knowing whether you have reached them. The result will be confusion, uncertainty, and the possible erosion of confidence in your decision to go.

Here's a list of the objectives most common among Americans going abroad to live. Check those that apply to you. Then put an "X" beside those that apply to your spouse if you feel they are different from your own. Have your spouse check the list too.

1. Advancement in job or profession

2. Challenge of the specific assignment overseas

3. Opportunity to make more money

4. Pressure from superiors

5. Desire to expand the experience of the family

6. Desire to experience an exotic, foreign place

7. Desire to learn another language and culture

8. Desire to keep up with colleagues and friends who have been overseas

9. Desire to get away from life in the United States

10. Need for a change

11. Desire to get away from something in personal or professional life

12. Hope that the new setting will solve something distressing in personal, professional, or family life

13. Hope that foreign experience will stop the drift, uncertainty, or pointlessness in your personal or professional life and give it new direction and meaning

14. Other

You've probably checked a number of motives, and that's okay. Plan to return to this list from time to time while you're abroad to test whether the goals you've identified as yours are being achieved.

For the moment, however, go back over the list carefully once more. Are there motivations on the list (or others inside you) that you were unwilling to recognize? Almost everyone who goes abroad has mixed motives, some of which he or she is not too comfortable with. But if these motives are present within you, they will inevitably influence your experience. It's better to get them out on the table than to suppress them. In the open they can be managed and probably transformed by talking with a close friend, discussing them with your spouse, or even getting the advice of a counselor. As long as you have your needs and goals clearly and honestly stated in your own mind and can establish your expectations realistically, they can do little harm in your life overseas, even if they are less idealistic than you might wish them to be.

11

On Becoming a Foreigner

You've often had the experience of encountering foreigners in the United States. Did any of them ever let down their hair and tell you how uncomfortable they felt being a foreigner? If so, you probably have a sense of what those feelings are. Now the tables are turned. Suddenly, *you're* the foreigner and you'll experience the inevitable discomfort yourself.

This discomfort will grow as the apparent similarities between you and your hosts are revealed as relatively superficial and the deeper differences become more and more a factor in your daily personal and professional life.

In your own country, you are surrounded by many things which define and reinforce your identity and role—who you are.

Some are symbols—like the country's flag, which expresses our national identity.

Some are the accoutrements of role—a briefcase, carpenter's tools, chalk and eraser, a business suit.

Some are people—the president (of your company or country), certain quintessential Americans, a special friend or mentor, a local store owner, your minister or rabbi.

Some are family—your immediate family members and the relatives who may stretch from coast to coast.

Some are places you enjoy or love—a favorite restaurant, a quiet park, your office, the den in your home, a place of amusement.

Some are physical landmarks—a building, a street, a monument, a mountain in the distance, an ocean shore, or the old homestead.

Although many of these may change—friends grow apart, open fields turn into industrial parks—those changes occur within a context that you understand and are a part of. You belong. The fundamental patterns in your relationships and surroundings are generally familiar and predictable.

Stop for a moment and think of the things in your life which mean the most to you—"home," "culture," "community," and "country"—which according to psychologists reinforce your cultural identity. Jot them down in the space below if you wish.

IDENTITY REINFORCEMENTS:

When we go overseas, most of these identity reinforcements are suddenly withdrawn; they are replaced with things which, at first, are all too foreign. But what is really foreign is *you*.

There is an important exception to this rule—if

you go *en famille,* you take with you a central piece of home identity. Family members may serve as a core support system for one another in confronting and sharing the excitements, frustrations, problems, and rewards of the overseas experience.

Even with your family, however, being a foreigner is a new and, at least for a time, an uncomfortable, even threatening experience. It can produce a persistent sense of insecurity vibrating just below the threshold of consciousness—something like a long-term, low-grade infection, not seriously disruptive but annoyingly debilitating. The best antidote is a strong sense of who you are.

In the next chapter we'll look at a few ways to neutralize the negative impact of being a foreigner.

12

A Strategy for Strangers

One of Robert Heinlein's science fiction novels has an intriguing title—*Stranger in a Strange Land*—which captures the essence of the cultural experience abroad.

What we're going to offer here is a strategy for a stranger entering a strange land. If strategies work in business, war, and politics, why not in your venture overseas?

One of the first things learned in a map-reading class is to orient the map. "Orienting the map" means to get the north indicator on the map pointing true north. The next step is to locate yourself on the map and make sure you know in which direction you are pointed.

But how?

Look ahead for a moment. Visualize yourself recently arrived, the settling-in process satisfactorily started. In what ways should you attempt to orient yourself after you are actually in-country? Here are a few suggestions:

1. *Start* with your apartment, home, office— whatever is your spatial center—and work out from there in more or less concentric circles.

   a. What places are in the immediate vicinity—stores, shops, services, offices, etc.?

   b. Who inhabits the places nearby? The poor? The rich? The middle class? Are they friendly, hostile, or neutral?

   c. Locate English speakers.

2. *Next, explore further* into the neighborhood nearby.

   a. Locate restaurants and other places where people gather.

   b. Locate transportation.

   c. Locate government offices—the post office, the police, schools, administrative offices.

3. *Begin to learn* the basic names and phrases that appear on the signs, the names of foods or services. Learn to read the street signs. Learn the monetary system.

4. *Look for the differences.* Are needs met differently here from the way they are at home? Are things organized differently? What's the logic or custom behind the naming of streets? Are there different combinations of food or other goods in the stores or markets? What goods are displayed most prominently? What does that tell you? What buildings stand out? How do you get a taxi? Pay on a bus? There is bound to be something vital to you that seems to be totally missing. Does this society ignore a basic human need? Don't panic. The need is probably met in a different way from what you're used to.

5. *Talk to people.* Identify friendly English speakers and develop an acquaintanceship. Don't be afraid to ask questions. Most people are very anxious to tell foreigners about their country. Go systematically into different stores and offices and strike up conversations with anyone who will talk with you. (See the next chapter, "Know Thy Host Country," for subjects to cover.)

6. *Accept the help of other Americans, but....* You will almost certainly encounter other Americans virtually the minute you arrive. You may have friends anxiously awaiting your plane. All to the good. Other Americans can provide you much information quickly. Other Americans and friendly host nationals, in fact, can help make your transition into the new society smoother than it might otherwise be.

But it is important to remember that living in another country stirs up complex emotions and responses. Each person's reactions are very nearly unique. Yours will be too. It is therefore important not to let your perception of your host country be filtered too much through the eyes and experience of other Americans. Accept their help and friendship but be wary of their opinions, especially if they focus excessively on the alleged shortcomings of their hosts. In short, gather information only from Americans who have a basically healthy and positive attitude toward the country and its people. You don't need other people's worn-out prejudices and stereotypes.

13

Know Thy Host Country

Your strategy will, of course, work perfectly. You will soon be settled in. You'll have a whole network of sources of information or, at least, willing conversationalists. You'll be partying with friends, exploring fascinating out-of-the-way places, and accomplishing great things at the office (if you're the jobholder in the family).

All you have to do now is sit back and enjoy, right?

Wrong.

It just isn't that easy. You have to put much more into it if you're going to get out of your overseas experience all that you can. Indeed, as with most things, you will derive from it a value more or less equal to the time, involvement, and commitment you put into it. But the effort will be worth it. Learning about a new country on site is a rewarding pursuit.

Of course, you will never feel you know all there is to know about the country. At first you'll feel desperately ignorant. To speed up the process you should consider adopting some sort of plan, like the one suggested below.

Before going on, however, let's consider *where* to gather your information.

Before You Go

There are friends and acquaintances who have been there and nationals of the country living in or visiting the United States. Your city or town may have an international hospitality center through which you can meet foreign visitors. The country's embassy (in Washington) will usually be helpful. Certainly its tourist office (normally in New York) will be. If there is a college or university near you, there is bound to be at least one professor who has studied the country and would be flattered to have his or her expertise called upon. And there may be a few students from the country who would be willing to talk with you or even visit your home.

After You Arrive

Of course you'll develop your network and your friends. In addition, there are in most countries all kinds of information available for tourists, some of it quite substantive. If you're in a large city, there will probably be a bookstore stocking books in English—with a good supply covering the host country and culture. Go browse. Look for magazines and newspapers edited in the country but printed in English. If you read the language, of course, a wealth of material will be available to you.

The best means of gathering information from people—whether they are Americans or host nationals—is to ask questions. Talk with people every chance you get, and don't hesitate to ask the questions for which you need answers.

It is disheartening to discover how little really adequate information is available in print about many of the countries and cultures around the world. If your country or destination is among them, take heart. It's more fun and educationally more sound to do it yourself. You'll be discovering what you need to know from the best possible source— the people who are there—and you may even be able to write the guidebook that will help those who follow you.

But that can wait. First you have to collect the information that's useful to you. There are at least nine important information-gathering areas.

1. *History.* Look for something brief unless you're a history nut. Don't get bogged down in a heavy tome that would put an insomniac to sleep.

2. *Basic factual information.* On natural resources, family organization, religion, art, political structure, etc. Appendix B includes a list of such subject areas.

3. *A human profile.* Develop a profile of an average host national the way we have done, in the course of this book, of an average mainstream American.

   For only a handful of countries is a really good profile already prepared and packaged. Yet the profile is the most useful of these devices for getting to know the host country because it contains the "people facts."

   You will probably have to experiment to find the best way to make up the profile, and it may take quite a while and a lot of digging. One approach is through the "Grandparent Exercise." Assume you are a grandparent in the host country. Then ask yourself what you would tell your grandchildren about the values, behaviors, and basic social processes of your country. Suggested topics for this exercise are listed in Appendix C.

4. *Specific do's and don't's for the stranger.* As you know, each culture has its own set of manners, expected behaviors, and unspoken rules. Find out what they are before going or as soon as possible after arriving.

5. *Present-day problems and current national affairs.* This kind of information is necessary to an intelligent understanding of what's going on around you. Learning about current affairs is one of the best ways to get a sense of how people evaluate events from different viewpoints and perspectives. In this process, collect your data and remember to withhold judgment until you're sure you understand what everything means.

6. *Problems you as an American are likely to encounter.* These are problems that are going to arise primarily out of what you bring with you, your cultural baggage. *Neither you nor the host culture is to blame,* however. You need particularly objective information to begin to solve these problems. Here again, other Americans are probably a good source for both the information and the solutions. But beware of emotion-laden biases.

Your best bet will be Americans who are essentially sympathetic to, yet able to be objective about, the country. Don't listen to those who make judgments about the host culture according to its deviation from American standards.

7. *How to meet your logistical needs.* American informants can help here too, though much personal exploration will probably be necessary. Some resources are listed in Appendix E, and a checklist of needed information appears in Appendix D. (This checklist is by no means exhaustive, but it will get you started.)

8. *Principal sights, monuments, and scenic areas.* There is a high correlation between those foreigners who function at their best overseas and those with the keenest interest in exploring the country to which they are assigned.

    A national of the country will probably be your best resource in this venture. Why not invite him or her along as a guide-companion?

9. *Identify the nation's heroes and heroines.* As Americans, we might expect someone who had come to live in the United States to know about George Washington or Abraham Lincoln (although we probably wouldn't ask). Familiarity with your hosts' myths, history, and famous men and women will endear you to them. This is the kind of name-dropping nobody minds.

14

Let's Play Q and A

Here is a list of basic questions[1] about your host country and culture. It is not intended to be an inclusive list. Many more questions will be suggested as you attempt to answer these. Nevertheless, when you have the answers to the following, you may consider yourself well beyond the beginner stage.

Go through the list now and write down the answers to as many as you can. Return to the list periodically, both as a guide and as a check on the progress of your quest for information.

1. What kind of government does your host country have? Can you name people prominent in the country's affairs (politics, athletics, religion, the arts, etc.)?

---

[1] Adapted from a list developed by Joan Wilson, Foreign Service Institute, U.S. Department of State. Another guide to what questions to ask when learning about another country and culture "on site" is: Bryan Grey, Ken Darrow, Dan Morrow, and Brad Palmquist, *Transcultural Study Guide* (Stanford, CA: Volunteers in Asia, 1975).

2. Who are the country's national heroes and heroines? Can you recognize the national anthem?

3. What is your host country's attitude toward trash? The environment? Conservation of resources?

4. Are other languages spoken besides the dominant language? What are the social and political implications of language usage?

5. What is the predominant religion? Is it a state religion? Are they tolerant of other religions? Have you read any of its sacred writings?

6. What are the most important religious observances and ceremonies? How regularly do people participate in them?

7. How are animals treated? Are they household pets? Which animals are household pets?

8. What are the most common forms of marriage ceremonies and celebrations?

9. What is the attitude toward divorce? Extramarital relations? Plural marriage?

10. What is the attitude toward gambling? Toward drinking? Toward drugs?

11. Do women work outside the home? In professional jobs?

12. Is the price asked for merchandise fixed or are customers expected to bargain? How is the bargaining conducted?

13. If, as a customer, you touch or handle merchandise for sale, will the storekeeper think you are knowledgeable? Inconsiderate? Within your rights? Completely outside your rights? Other?

14. How do people organize their daily activities? What is the normal meal schedule? Is there a daytime rest period? What is the customary time for visiting friends?

15. What foods are most popular and how are they prepared? Who sits down together for meals? Who is served first?

16. What things are taboo in this society?

17. What is the usual dress for women? For men? Are slacks and/or shorts worn? If so, on what occasions? Do teenagers wear jeans?

18. Are there special privileges of age and/or sex? What kinds of group social activities are there? Are they divided by sex?

19. If you are invited to dinner, should you arrive early? On time? Late? If late, how late? Is being on time an important consideration in keeping doctor's appointments? Business appointments?

20. On what occasions would you present (or accept) gifts from people in the country? What kinds of gifts would you exchange?

21. Do some flowers have a particular significance?

22. How do people greet one another? Shake hands? Embrace or kiss? How do they take leave of one another? What does any variation from the usual greeting or leave-taking signify?

23. Can women vote? Travel alone? Drive a car?

24. What are the important holidays? How is each observed?

25. What are the favorite leisure and recreational activities of adults? Children? Teenagers? Are

the sexes separated in these activities? Where are these activities held?

26. What is the attitude toward adoption? Beggars? The homeless?

27. What kinds of television programs are shown? What social purposes do they serve?

28. What is the normal work schedule? Is it important to be on time?

29. How will your financial position and living conditions compare with those of the majority of people living in this country?

30. How are children disciplined at home? At school? Are they catered to?

31. Are children usually present at social occasions? At ceremonial occasions? If they are not present, how are they cared for in the absence of their parents?

32. How does this society observe children's "coming of age"? Are boys preferred over girls?

33. What kind of local public transportation is available? Do all classes of people use it?

34. Who has the right of way in traffic? Vehicles? Animals? Pedestrians?

35. Is military training compulsory?

36. Are the largest newspapers generally friendly in their attitude toward the United States?

37. What is the history of the relationship between this country and the United States?

38. How many people have emigrated from this country to the United States? Other countries? Are many doing so at present?

39. Are there many American expatriates living in this country? Where do they live?

40. What kinds of health services are available? Where are they located?

41. What are the common home remedies for minor ailments? Where can medicines be purchased?

42. Is education free? Compulsory? Are girls encouraged to attend high school? College?

43. In schools, are children segregated by race? By caste? By class? By sex?

44. What kinds of schools are considered best? Public? Private? Parochial?

45. In schools, how important is learning by rote?

46. Is there a strong belief in fate?

47. Where are the important universities of the country? If university education is sought abroad, to what countries and universities do students go?

15

Speaking of Learning the Language

Many people faced with a new assignment overseas vow, in a state of high anticipation, that they'll not only go and explore this faraway and exotic land, but that they'll learn the language as well. They will get the books and start tomorrow.

For many that tomorrow never comes. A smattering of phrases is all that results from the abundant good intentions and however many months or years spent abroad.

Many people judge themselves too harshly when they fail to learn the language. The resulting guilt, however, probably does more harm than the failure itself. There are a number of reasons why people don't learn the language of their host country. One is that, particularly for an adult, learning another language from scratch is just plain hard; for some, agony. It takes time and effort and leaves you open to embarrassment, if not humiliation. It's a forbidding prospect to many people.

What about you? Should you try to learn the language of your new country? That's a question only you can answer, but it's one you should face squarely.

If English is widely used or if your work setting or living environment is an English-speaking one, you can probably manage without the language. But if you're going to countries like Libya or Uruguay or Indonesia, where little English is spoken, it's another matter.

Having just given you permission not to feel guilty if you decide not to learn the local language, we would like to badger you a little about the value of doing so. Although learning another language as an adult may be one of the most difficult tasks you've ever undertaken it will be worth every ounce of effort it takes. There is a high correlation between those who learn the language and those who adjust best to, and function most effectively in, the country.

The ability to speak just a few phrases expressing the common courtesies to the people you are living among says a great deal. In fact, it speaks volumes; above all: "I respect you and your culture and I'm doing my level best to learn all I can about it."

The fact that Americans have a poor reputation as foreign language learners is not something to be proud of. Most people born in the United States are monolingual and many have the attitude: "If they want to speak to me, let them learn English." Fortunately for us, English is the most widely spoken second language in the world, but that's a poor substitute for being able to talk to a person in his/her native tongue.

Actually, Americans have a rich linguistic background, brought with them as immigrants. Many have grown up in bilingual homes, speaking two languages from childhood. But this richness of experience has declined as the country strove to assimilate immigrant families into the English-speaking society. We are now slowly realizing that the child who learns two (or more) languages from early childhood is fortunate. Even in the business world, Americans are recognizing that the company representative who is fluent in both English and the language of the country of assignment, all else being equal, is worth far more than the one who must make do with English only. There is even an aphorism frequently heard in the corporate world today: "If you're going to buy, you can do it in your own language. If you want to sell, you'd better do it in the local language."

Once you've decided to make the commitment, don't hold back. Put the effort into it that is needed. Also be assured that *anything* you learn will be of value, even if it never comes easy. Words, phrases, fragments of sentences—understood or spoken—open windows on the society, revealing the richness that lies within any culture. Don't worry about what the host nationals think of your modest, fumbling efforts. Most will be delighted.

Every language has words and phrases that cannot be readily translated, only explained. Such phrases are carriers of culture because they represent special ways a culture has developed to view some aspect of human existence. Through language people classify the world around them. Finding out how one group of people, one culture, makes those classifications is one of the most enjoyable and rewarding aspects of living overseas. It would be sad to miss these through an unwillingness to take at least a stab at learning the language.

A number of books have been written precisely to assist in making the language-learning process more comprehensible and easier to manage. Look them up and spend a few hours browsing.[1]

---

[1] Some of the best are: Donald N. Larson and William A. Smalley, *Becoming Bilingual: A Guide to Language Learning* (South Pasadena, CA: Practical Anthropology, 1974); Thomas and Elizabeth Brewster, *Language Acquisition Made Practical: Field Methods for Language Learning* (Colorado Springs, CO: Lingua House, 1976); Terry Marshall, *The Whole World Guide to Language Learning* (Yarmouth, ME: Intercultural Press, 1990); and H. Douglas Brown, *Breaking the Language Barrier* (Yarmouth ME: Intercultural Press, 1991).

16

Getting Down to the Nitty-Gritty

Now it's time to get down to the nitty-gritty, to ask what it is that really bothers Americans about living in a foreign country and what it is that most bothers host nationals about working closely with Americans.

What Bothers Americans?

At an institute on intercultural communication held at Stanford University some years ago, a group of experienced cross-cultural specialists brainstormed the first question and came up with the following:

- Language barriers
- Lack of mobility
- Indirectness
- Formality, protocol, rank
- The slow pace of life
- Lack of conveniences

- Social customs and expectations
- Alcohol and drug problems
- Family problems
- Health problems
- Emotional instability

Many of these problems are obvious or have been touched upon earlier and need no further comment. Several, however, deserve an additional word or two.

Lack of mobility

In societies with tighter controls over political activity and movement within the country, Americans often get a feeling of imposed isolation. In some countries there may be severe restrictions on freedom of movement for women or for teenagers. Many non-Western countries have radically different concepts of the way males and females should behave toward each other in public. Frustration may result if basic transportation services are inadequate.

In some instances psychological immobility may be felt, especially in countries where the freedom to discuss issues openly, to engage in lively political discussions, or to argue your opinions in a friendly way with the nationals is restricted. All of these can have the effect of making an American feel unduly hemmed in.

Indirectness

In some cultures American directness is a source of irritation. In some societies confrontations are avoided at all costs. This can confuse and trouble an outspoken American.

Sense of time and pace of life

For action-oriented Americans it is not easy to adjust to a slower pace. Nor do they appreciate putting up with red tape, bureaucratic delays, and missed appointments.

Lack of conveniences

These will include many luxuries which you may have come to expect as necessary for the full enjoyment of life: your favorite TV programs and sports events, adequate heating or air conditioning, pure water right from the tap, special foods, modern appliances, etc., etc.

Just remember, it's a trade-off. For everything you are forced to give up, you will be able to discover, if you're open to it, some new dimension of life you have not experienced before. For example, you may have to give up some familiar convenience to work in Brazil, but it will be more than compensated for by the lesson in "loosening up" which Brazil has to teach you.

Alcohol and drug problems

Under the stresses of life in a new environment, some people turn to drink. When it becomes excessive, counseling and closer attention to the psychological impact of the cross-cultural experience are called for. At this point culture shock is transformed from a minor ailment to a major sickness.

The easy availability of drugs and the harsh drug laws in some countries have created explosive situations for teenagers, who are at a vulnerable age anyway.

Most families do well overseas but, given the natural stresses, the family unit can become a tinderbox demanding careful attention to see that the needs of all its members are met.

Family problems

Marital and other family problems which existed

prior to departure will rarely improve under the strains of overseas living. Indeed, they will almost certainly get worse. Even the most stable of families can expect new stresses. Solve your marital and family problems before you leave home.

What Bothers Host Nationals?

Now to the second question: What is it that most bothers host nationals about working with Americans?

Here's a list gathered from a variety of sources over the years:

1. They expect to accomplish more in the local environment than is reasonable.
2. They are insensitive to local customs and cultural norms.
3. They resist working through normal administrative channels.
4. They often take credit for joint efforts.
5. They think they have all the right answers.
6. They are too abrupt and task-oriented; insensitive to the feelings of others.

It may sound harsh, but it's the way Americans too often have been perceived. It's the stuff of stereotypes which only you and others like you can sweep away.

In the months ahead, return to this checklist occasionally. Cultural behaviors are so ingrained and so difficult to recognize in ourselves that we need ways of periodically testing whether or not we're still on the right track.

17

The Handyman's Guide to Intercultural Communication

We're not trying to develop experts in intercultural communication. It's a hard skill to master completely. Also, it will come to you little by little. By the time you're ready to return home, if you've had your antennae out, you'll be a pretty good handyman or handywoman at communicating across cultures.

What we *can* do is introduce you to some of the processes and alert you to the basic dynamics of intercultural communication.[1]

---

[1] The best general books currently available on intercultural communication are: Larry Samovar and Richard Porter, *Communication between Cultures* (Belmont, CA: Wadsworth, 1991); Larry Samovar and Richard Porter, *Intercultural Communication: A Reader* (Belmont, CA: Wadsworth, 1993); Gary Weaver, *Culture, Communication and Conflict* (Needham Heights, MA: Ginn, 1994); Richard Brislin, *Understanding Culture's Influence on Behavior* (Orlando, FL: Harcourt Brace Jovanovich, 1993); Richard Brislin, Kenneth Cushner, Craig Cherrie, and Mahealani Yong, *Intercultural Interactions: A Practical Guide* (Newbury Park, CA: Sage, 1986).

When you're talking to someone, how often are you aware of the *process* of communication that is taking place?

If you're like most of us, the answer is—virtually never (unless it breaks down!).

Why not?

One reason is that we have been doing it for so long (at least since the doctor slapped us on the rear a few seconds after we were ejected from the womb) and because it seems so simple and natural.

But there's another reason. Communication takes place in the medium of one's culture, which facilitates and reinforces it but also hides it. It's like one of those pictures in children's fun books where figures of animals are buried in a scene and the kids have to find them. Communication is buried in our own cultural scene and is difficult to extract and look at.

Not so abroad. Communication becomes a major issue. We stumble over it continuously—even if we have learned the language. That's because not only do languages vary from country to country, but so do communication styles and, especially, codes of *nonverbal* communication (more on that in a moment). Also, words don't always translate from one language to another as precisely as we would like.

Perception is at the heart of intercultural communication. Down deep, we assume that under normal circumstances we all think about and perceive the world in basically the same way and, therefore, that whatever I say will mean the same to you as it does to me.

Fair assumption?

Of course not.

We misperceive, misinterpret, and misunderstand each other all the time, even when we share many values, attitudes, beliefs, and ways of doing, be-ing, and thinking.

Doesn't it stand to reason that there are going to be greater possibilities of misperceiving and mis-understanding when in a foreign country?

It does indeed.

Look at the illustration below. If there are people with you, let them look at it too. Study it for a mo-ment and then go on to the following page.

1. What do you see?
2. If there are others with you, what do they see?
3. Do you and the others see something different?

You probably saw a woman. If you were a young man about town would you be interested in getting a date with her? Did you by any chance see more than one woman? If not, go back and look again. Study the picture carefully. Talk about it with someone else if possible.

Shown in the picture are the heads and shoulders of both an old woman and a young woman, though normally you can only see one at a time.

For some people, seeing both women even in sequence is very difficult.

Which brings us to:

Point 1

Our perceptions play tricks on us. Even though we know intellectually that this is true, in our everyday lives we assume an objectivity and a reliability that is not borne out by events. Things are not always as they seem.

Research on responses to this picture has turned up something else interesting: that young people usually see the young woman and older people see the old woman.

Which brings us to:

Point 2

We are selective in what we perceive (psychologists call it "selective perception"). In fact, most of what we are seeing, hearing, smelling, tasting, or feeling at any moment is screened out by our conscious minds.

We tend to perceive consciously only that which is important to us.

But what, for the most part, determines what it is that we consider important? It is our enculturation, our cultural training.

This culturally determined perceptual set is the great steamer trunk in the cultural baggage we haul abroad with us.

When the picture of the two women (sometimes called "The Ambiguous Lady") is shown to a *group* of people, those who can't see both women are subjected to much good-natured teasing and joking and end up feeling a little stupid.

Which brings us to:

Point 3

When you're in a situation (your host culture, for instance) *where everyone perceives something in ways you don't, you feel stupid,* which can be pretty depressing. Antidote: get comfortable with feeling a little stupid when you're overseas. It happens to everyone. You'll eventually find out what's going on, and in the meantime you'll save a lot of useless anguish.

Is there anything you can *do* (being a good, action-oriented American) to get yourself ready to charm your hosts abroad with intercultural communication skills?

There certainly is.

Find an acquaintance who is willing to carry on an experimental conversation with you—a neighbor, an office colleague, or perhaps a stranger on the plane—it shouldn't be a family member or a close friend. Here are the rules of the experiment.

1. Pick a subject of some importance to you (a political issue, juvenile delinquency, stock market investments, sex, taxes, etc.).

2. Discuss it for two minutes without interruption while your partner listens.

3. At the end of the two minutes ask your partner to summarize as accurately as possible what you said.

4. If the summary is inaccurate in *any* way, correct it and ask your partner to resummarize it.

5. Continue this until your partner has repeated your meaning exactly.

6. Reverse the roles and repeat the exercise.

What does this experiment prove? Mainly, that it is hard to listen well. Too simple? Not at all.

Listening is something of an art. A high percentage of miscommunication occurs because the listener either isn't listening or is listening to the words, not the meaning. The question of effective listening (or "active" listening, as it is sometimes called) becomes critical when talking with people from other cultures.

When you are in your own culture there are dozens of little cues which help convey meaning—gestures, facial expressions, body motions ("body language"), eye contact, voice inflection—all of which in the speaker occur automatically and are interpreted immediately by the listener without conscious thought. We've all learned, for example, that "catching the person's eye" is important in some situations. In similar situations abroad, direct eye contact may be considered impolite or disrespectful. It may, however, be entirely correct in a different context, and *that* may seem strange to you.

Overseas, many if not most of these nonverbal methods of elaborating and reinforcing the meaning of a verbal message are different, sometimes very different. Combine this with the fact that the meaning must be interpreted from a different cultural perspective and you have the obvious proposition:

> Overseas you have to listen two or three times as hard to people in order to find out what they really mean.

There's another way to help you get at real meaning when you're abroad. This one's basically easy, but will take some courage.

Ask the person you're talking with what he or she means.

Another oversimplification? We don't think so. If you want the technical term, it's called "perception-checking." The way to find out if you've got something straight—if you've "perceived" it accurately—is to check it out, to ask if something meant what you think it did.

It takes courage because overseas you may feel stupid or embarrassed to do so. The challenge is to find a way to check your perceptions which does not make you feel uncomfortable and which is not offensive to your hosts.

One of the reasons we give all this attention to communication is because it is central to building cross-cultural relationships. And building relationships with host nationals is, in many respects, what it's all about.

Much of your effectiveness on the job and satisfaction in the overseas living experience will depend on how well you build working and social relationships with host nationals.

Skillful intercultural communication is a medium for finding out what expectations your hosts have of you and of getting across your expectations of them. It is a means of creating trust and communicating your sincerity and goodwill. It is a method of anticipating problems and solving those which arise. It is a channel for reaching out and establishing links with people.

18

Culture Shock: Occupational Hazard of Overseas Living

In preparing for the big move, you've probably had—or will soon have—all the vaccinations, inoculations, and shots required. These will keep you safe from the dread diseases that can still be found in some parts of the world.

There is no vaccination, however, for one condition you are likely to encounter—culture shock. In all probability, the doctor who gave you your other shots wouldn't even have been able to talk intelligently about it.

Culture shock is the term used to describe the more pronounced reactions to the psychological disorientation most people experience when they move for an extended period of time into a culture markedly different from their own. Today, nearly everyone has at least heard the phrase "culture shock." This was not true sixteen years ago when the first editon of this book was published. Well-read people who have never ventured out of their own country are now as aware of the term as the most experienced of world travelers. There remains, however, a great deal of confusion regarding just exactly what it is, why it happens, and how to get yourself safely through it. This chapter and the next address the fine points of this experience and will hopefully move you from thinking of culture shock as a kind of illness—which is the most common perception of it—to seeing it as a learning experience and a natural occurrence in the process of adjusting to a culture that is different from your own. Culture shock can cause intense discomfort, often accompanied by hyperirritability, bitterness, resentment, homesickness, and depression. In some cases distinct physical symptoms of psychosomatic illness occur.

For some people the bout with culture shock is brief and hardly noticeable. These are usually people whose personalities provide them with a kind of natural immunity. For most of us, however, culture shock is something we'll have to deal with over a period of at least several months, possibly a year or more.

In a sense, culture shock is the occupational hazard of overseas living through which one has to be willing to go in order to have the pleasures of experiencing other countries and cultures in depth.

All of us have known frustration at one time or another. Although related and similar in emotional content, culture shock is different from frustration. Frustration is always traceable to a specific action or cause and goes away when the situation is remedied or the cause is removed.

Some of the common causes of frustration are:

- the ambiguity of a particular situation
- the actual situation not matching preconceived ideas of what it would be like

- unrealistic goals
- not being able to see results
  —because of the enormity of the need
  —because of the nature of the work
  —because of the shortness of time of one's
    involvement
- using the wrong methods to achieve objectives (i.e., methods which are inappropriate to the new culture)

Frustration may be uncomfortable, but it is generally short-lived as compared to culture shock.

Culture shock has two quite distinctive features:

1. It does not result from a specific event or series of events. It comes instead from the experience of encountering ways of doing, organizing, perceiving, or valuing things which are different from yours and which *threaten* your basic, unconscious belief that your encultured customs, assumptions, values, and behaviors are "right."

2. It does not strike suddenly or have a single principal cause. Instead it is cumulative. It builds up slowly, from a series of small events which are difficult to identify.

Culture shock comes from:

- being cut off from the cultural cues and known patterns with which you are familiar—especially the subtle, indirect ways you normally have of expressing feelings. All the nuances and shades of meaning that you understand instinctively and use to make your life comprehensible are suddenly taken from you.
- living and/or working over an extended period of time in a situation that is ambiguous.

- having your own values (which you had heretofore considered as absolutes) brought into question—which yanks your moral rug out from under you.
- being continually put into a position in which you are expected to function with maximum skill and speed but where the rules have not been adequately explained.

Regarding being cut off from your own cultural cues, Kalvero Oberg, the man first credited with diagnosing culture shock, says:

> These signs and clues include the thousand and one ways in which we orient ourselves to the situations of daily life: when to shake hands and what to say when we meet people, when and how to give tips, how to give orders to servants, how to make purchases, when to accept and when to refuse invitations, when to take statements seriously and when not....[1]

These are just a few examples, but they show how *pervasive* is the disorientation out of which culture shock emerges.

The Progressive Stages of Culture Shock

As indicated above, culture shock progresses slowly. One's first reaction to different ways of doing things may be "How quaint!" When it becomes clear that the differences are not simply quaint, an effort is frequently made to dismiss them by pointing out the fundamental *sameness* of human nature. After

---

[1] Kalvero Oberg, "Cultural Shock: Adjustment to new cultural environments." *Practical Anthropology* 7 (1960): 177-82.

all, people are really basically the same under the skin, aren't they?

Eventually, the focus shifts to the *differences* themselves, sometimes to such an extent that they seem to be overwhelming. The final stage comes when the differences are narrowed down to a few of the most troubling and then are blown up out of all proportion. (For Americans, standards of cleanliness, attitudes toward punctuality, and the value of human life tend to loom especially large.)

By now the sojourner is in an acute state of distress. The host culture has become the scapegoat for the natural difficulties inherent in the cross-cultural encounter. Culture shock has set in.

Of course, no two people experience culture shock in exactly the same way. Some are less affected than others, but there is an interesting pattern which you may observe in yourself and in others' reactions. In situations in the host culture which cause culture shock reactions, you may notice that you have a tendency either to withdraw from the unpleasant situation, or you may become aggressive and strike back. We all tend to react in one way or the other. A few people try both approaches, but people generally favor the approach which best fits their personality.

Reactions to Culture Shock Situations

The chart on the following page lists the multiple reactions which people normally have to culture shock.

Overall Symptoms	Withdrawal Symptoms	Aggressive Symptoms
Anxiety	Physical and/or psychological withdrawal	Compulsive eating
Homesickness	Spending excessive amounts of time reading	Compulsive drinking
Helplessness	Need for excessive amounts of sleep	Exaggerated cleanliness
Boredom	Only seeing other Americans or Westerners	Irritability
Depression	Avoiding contact with host nationals	Family tensions
Fatigue	Short attention span	Marital stress
Confusion	Diminished productivity	Excessive chauvinism
Self-doubt	Loss of ability to work or study effectively	Stereotyping
Feelings of inadequacy	Quitting and returning to your home country early	Hostility toward host nationals
Unexplained fits of weeping		Verbal aggressiveness
Paranoia		Physical aggressiveness
Physical ailments and psychosomatic illnesses		Deciding to stay but permanently hating the country and its people

Not everyone will experience a severe case of culture shock, nor will all the symptoms be observed in any single individual. Many people sail through culture shock with relative ease, only now and again experiencing the more serious reactions. But many others don't. For them it is important to know that 1) the above responses can occur, 2) culture shock is in some degree inevitable, and 3) their reactions are emotional and not easily subject to rational management. This knowledge should give those individuals a better understanding of what is happening to them and buttress their resolve to work at hastening recovery.

Before we examine what you can do to counteract culture shock, let's spend a few minutes fitting it into the whole overseas experience.

Some time ago intercultural specialists began to recognize that there were distinct stages of personal adjustment which virtually everyone who lived abroad went through (no matter where they came from or what country they were living in).

These stages are:

1. Initial euphoria
2. Irritability and hostility
3. Gradual adjustment
4. Adaptation or biculturalism

1. Initial euphoria

Most people begin their new assignment with great expectations and a positive mindset. If anything, they come with expectations which are too high and attitudes which are too positive toward the host country and toward their own prospective experiences in it. At this point, anything new is intriguing and exciting. But, for the most part, it is the *similarities* which stand out. The newcomer is usually impressed with how people everywhere are really very much alike.

This period of euphoria may last from a week or two to a month, but the letdown is inevitable. You've reached the end of the first stage.

2. Irritability and hostility

Gradually, your focus turns from the similarities to the *differences* and these differences, which suddenly seem to be everywhere, are troubling. You blow up little, seemingly insignificant difficulties into major catastrophes. This is the stage generally identified as culture shock, and you may experience any of the symptoms listed in the chart on page 92.

3. Gradual adjustment

The crisis is over and you are on your way to recovery. This step may come so gradually that, at first, you will be unaware it's even happening. Once you begin to orient yourself and are able to interpret some of the subtle cultural clues and cues which passed by unnoticed earlier, the culture seems more familiar. You *become more comfortable in it* and feel less isolated from it.

Gradually, too, your sense of humor returns and you realize the situation is not hopeless after all.

4. Adaptation and biculturalism

Full recovery will result in an ability to *function in two cultures* with confidence. You will even find a great many customs, ways of doing and saying things, and personal attitudes which you enjoy— indeed, to which you have in some degree acculturated—and which you will definitely miss when you pack up and return home. In fact, you can expect to experience "reverse culture shock" upon your return to the United States (See Postscript 1 beginning on page 117.) In some cases, particularly where a person has adjusted exceptionally well to the host country, reverse culture shock may cause greater distress than the original culture shock.

The interesting thing about culture shock is that there are routinely not one but *two* low points and, even more interestingly, they will accommodate themselves to the amount of time you intend to spend in the host country! That is, they will spread themselves out if you're going to stay for a longer period or contract if your initial assignment is for a shorter time. You can't say that's not accommodating!

A graphic illustration of the "adjustment curve" can look something like that appearing on the following page.

Culture Shock Cycle

For a Two-Year Assignment

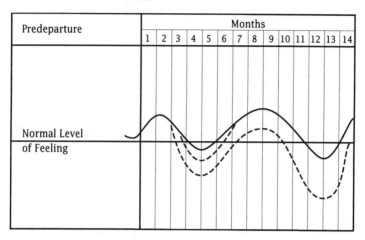

Predeparture	Months													
	1	2	3	4	5	6	7	8	9	10	11	12	13	14

Normal Level
of Feeling

How long will culture shock last?

As we have suggested, that varies with the length of your assignment. But it also depends to some extent on you and your resiliency. You can expect a letup after the first dip, but be prepared for the second downturn, which will probably be somewhat more severe.

Stop a moment and consider what you can do on your own to combat the onset and alleviate the effects of culture shock. What we have written so far in this book holds the key.

The next chapter offers our suggestions for working your way through culture shock.

19

Responding to Culture Shock

Granted that culture shock is virtually inevitable in some degree and that there are no magic charms to escape it altogether. There are, nevertheless, things you can do, positive steps you can take to minimize the impact—and the sooner you take them, the better.

Here's our prescription for action:

1. Realize that, in fact, practically everybody who goes overseas for a substantial period of time experiences culture shock in some form and/or to some degree. It's natural and not a sign that you're deficient or strange—and you'll live through it as thousands of others have.

2. Be ready for the lesson culture shock teaches. Culture is a survival mechanism which tells its members not only that their ways of doing things are right but also that they are superior. Culture shock stems from an in-depth encounter with another culture in which you learn to the contrary that there are *different*

ways of doing things that are neither wrong nor inferior. It teaches a lesson that cannot be learned as effectively by any other means: that one's own culture does not possess the single right way, best way, or even a uniformly better way of providing for human needs and enjoyments. Believing it does is a kind of imprisonment—from which the experience of culture shock, as painful as it may be, can liberate you.

3. Pack your copy of *Survival Kit for Overseas Living* and reread it when you're feeling down or uncertain about what is happening.

4. Return to chapter 13, "Know Thy Host Country," and pursue your information gathering assiduously. Go back to "Let's Play Q and A" and search out the answers you missed before. Develop a structured plan and daily schedule for doing your research and use all the native informants, sympathetic expatriates, and helpful books you can find as sources.

5. Select one or two areas of interest and investigate them more thoroughly than the other topics. If you are a fan of American football, for example, don't just sit around and grouse about missing the weekly games. Cultivate an interest in their football—soccer—or other national sports.

6. Begin (if you haven't done so already) consciously to look for logical reasons behind everything in the host culture which seems strange, difficult, confusing, or threatening. Take every aspect of your experience and look at it from their perspective. Search for patterns and interrelationships. You may be sur-

prised to find that the pieces fit together once you discover where they go. Relax your grip on your own culture a little in the process. There's no way you can lose it any more than you could forget your knowledge of English by learning another language.

7. Try to trace every "strange" action you observe in your new culture to its underlying value or values. An illustration in reverse, out of our own culture, will make the point. An Egyptian visitor to the United States was shocked at what he witnessed, firsthand, in the Air and Space Museum gift shop in Washington, D.C. There, he saw a young American mother squatting to bring herself down to more or less the eye level of what he took to be her six-year-old son. He overheard her saying to him, "Now, Tommy, if you buy that model airplane now, then you're not going to have enough money to buy a Coke when your sister wants to stop and have a Coke later in the morning, and then you're going to be very unhappy." He said he was shocked. No Egyptian mother would ever have said such a thing to her vacationing son. In the first place, the Egyptian mother would not have given the little boy "his own" money to manage; nor, when he failed to spend it for what the mother thought he should, would she intervene to teach him how best to spend it. The Egyptian mother would have held on to the money, then when her son wanted the model airplane, she would have bought it for him; then later, when he and his sister wanted a Coke, she would have bought them a Coke; then when they wanted something else, she would have bought them whatever else they wanted. They

were, after all, on a holiday; and they weren't poor or they wouldn't have been able to go on vacation. But he could see that it was absolutely "natural" for the American mother to act the way she did. And from this enlightening observation, he was able to identify several American values in action:

- Independence
- Self-help and individual responsibility
- Future orientation
- Delayed gratification
- Control over oneself and one's environment

In the same way, the interactions you observe in the foreign culture can reveal that country's values—provided you are as skilled as our Egyptian visitor in analyzing what lies behind what you see.

8. Make a list of all the *positive* things you can identify about your present situation. (Ignore the negative—which you've probably been concentrating on too much anyway.) Then tack the list up somewhere where you'll see it during the course of your day.

9. Avoid those Americans or other foreigners who are in a permanent state of culture shock and who spend their days seeking company to commiserate with. Finding new people to infect with their illness is the only way they have of proving that their negative analysis of the host country is correct. Consequently, they wait for each incoming boatload of Yankees to pounce on in order to convince them of the "stupidity of the natives." Avoid these people like the plague. The sickness they are

attempting to spread is far worse than a simple case of culture shock.

10. Don't succumb to the temptation to disparage the host culture yourself. Resist making jokes and denigrating comments ("Well, what else would you expect from these people?"). They only reinforce your beleaguered sense of self or shaky feelings of superiority and slow down the process of adaptation and of recapturing the true feelings of worth you are searching for. Avoid other people who make such jokes too. There is always one (or more) in every gathering of foreigners who will trade on jokes that denigrate the local culture, but like racial jokes back home, this type of humor is not worthy of being listened to.

11. On the other hand, work at maintaining a healthy sense of humor. Especially, be ready to laugh at yourself. It's one of the best antidotes to culture shock there is. Making silly mistakes because of your unfamiliarity with the culture may cause you to feel foolish or childish, but the embarrassment will pass. Share your gaffes with family and friends and get them out of your system with a good laugh.

12. Find an American who has been there longer, gone through culture shock, and has a positive attitude toward the host country, and use this person as a sounding board to help you get some perspective on the experience you are having.

13. Make friends with host nationals and try to develop a deeper, more intimate relationship with one or two of them. Discuss with them the problems you've been having, taking care

to present them in a way that doesn't sound like you're criticizing their culture. It is a truism that Americans who spend their time associating only with other Americans or other Westerners never do adjust to the host country.

14. When you look for advice, focus on how you are feeling—what is going on inside you—rather than on what you consider the *causes* of your problems, especially when you're inclined to think they lie in what is wrong in the host culture.

15. As you adjust to and function more comfortably within the value system of your host country, don't worry that you may lose your own values. This is a thought that comes quite naturally at some point or other to most people who live abroad. Your values are much deeper and more permanent than that. To act according to the customs of your host country (when and where it is appropriate) does not make you less of an American. It only makes you more comfortable and enables you to feel more at home.

16. Keep busy; keep active; keep your mind occupied. Don't sit around and feel sorry for yourself.

17. During the deepest plunges into culture shock, take a trip—get away to a scenic spot or a nearby country. When you return, be open to having good "coming back home" feelings.

18. Prepare some kind of presentation about the United States for your hosts, using slides, film, or some other kinds of visuals (you will have to prepare for this eventuality before

you leave home). Become an "unofficial ambassador"[1] whose mission it is to correct some of the many misconceptions which replays of *Beverly Hills 90210, Baywatch,* and *NYPD Blue* have created in people's minds overseas.

19. Even during the worst times—and especially at the worst times—have faith that you will work your way through culture shock to the brighter days that lie ahead—even if you do nothing but wait. Effective cross-cultural adaptation has a way of sneaking up on you as you accumulate bit by bit the knowledge you need.

20. If your spouse has accompanied you but is not working outside the home, be especially concerned about his/her welfare. Nonworking spouses can soon become bored and dissatisfied if they are not challenged to get out and explore the new environment.

There you have it: a 20-point program to get you safely through culture shock and to make sure that the rewards which come with the overseas experience will be yours to relive for the rest of your and your children's lives.

---

[1] An excellent book called *Citizen Ambassadors* by Charles T. Vetter and published by Brigham Young University in Provo, Utah, will help you develop your own answers to the often pointed and sometimes embarrassing questions you are likely to be asked about the United States when you are overseas.

20

Skills That Make a Difference

Some people seem to take to another culture more naturally than others. And some foreign cultures seem to be easier for Americans to adjust to than others. But there are certain skills or traits which you may have—or, with a little effort, may develop—which will facilitate your more rapid adjustment.

Before going on, jot down in the space below some of the skills—they are usually attitudes, ways of responding, and styles of behaving—which you think might be most helpful in the overseas adjustment process.

SKILLS:

Here are the skills which our experience has shown to be the most important:

- Tolerance for ambiguity
- Low goal/task orientation
- Open-mindedness
- Nonjudgmentalness
- Empathy
- Communicativeness
- Flexibility; adaptability
- Curiosity
- Sense of humor
- Warmth in human relationships
- Motivation
- Self-reliance
- Strong sense of self
- Tolerance for differences
- Perceptiveness
- Ability to fail

Add to these any of yours which we did not list. Then on a scale of one (low) to five (high), rate yourself in each of these characteristics. Write the number beside each one and total them. If you scored less than 55, you've got some work to do.

Now circle the traits you think are the *most* important (or guess what our choices are—it'll be no surprise that we're going to tell you).

Our choices:

1. Sense of humor
2. Low goal/task orientation
3. Ability to fail

A *sense of humor* is important because there is going to be much to weep or get angry or annoyed or embarrassed or discouraged about. No matter how many of the other traits you have, the ability to laugh things off will be the ultimate weapon against despair.

Americans abroad too often undertake *tasks* that are unrealistic and set goals for themselves that are unattainable. It is one of the major causes of failure. To the extent that you set your goals too high and refuse to adjust them to the realities of what can actually be accomplished in a foreign environment, you're going to be disappointed. Experience shows that Americans who are less goal-oriented or task-driven and more able to relax and ride with events tend to be more effective and enjoy themselves more overseas.

The ability to tolerate *failure* is critical because: 1) everyone fails at something overseas; it is absolutely built-in, 2) the highest stars in the American firmament of values are "achievement" and "success," and 3) the American most likely to be selected to go overseas is the person who has been most successful at home. Some people sent abroad will have virtually never experienced failure. If, in addition, they have little tolerance for it, they are in for trouble as are those who work for or live with them.

One of the largest international cultural exchange organizations in the United States (AFS International/Intercultural Programs) uses "a sense of humor" and "the ability to fail" as principal selection criteria for the thousands of people they choose for international exchanges.

21

Husbands, Wives and Children

In many, even most, cultures, the roles people play in their daily life—that of wife or husband, eldest son, or grandmother, for example—are much more clearly and rigidly defined than they are in the United States. So far this survival kit has dealt only with the general sorts of adaptation problems which any American citizen living abroad can expect to encounter. Now we turn to the special problems men, women, or children have living in a foreign country.

Husbands

Unfair though it is, men receive preferential treatment almost everywhere in the world—in the Middle East, in all of Asia and Latin America, even in Western Europe—yet an expatriate man will not lack problems.

A man often feels caught in the middle. In most cases of the family going abroad, it is the man whose company, organization, or agency has sent them abroad; therefore he feels responsible, particularly if anyone in the family is experiencing adjustment problems.

At the office, too, he may be the man in the middle. He is likely to be managing a staff whose culture and language are unfamiliar, and he finds himself either trying to impose his ways upon them or attempting—clumsily at first—to adapt to theirs. At the same time, he has to serve as liaison with a headquarters office thousands of miles away where his superiors typically have little comprehension of, or sympathy for, the cultural chasm separating the two operations.

Even if the man is not a workaholic in the United States, he may become one overseas just to function adequately in the new environment. The result, of course, is that he spends less time than usual with his wife and children who, because of their own adjustment difficulties, probably need more, not less, of his presence.

Even the male college student, without the burdens of organizational responsibility (or, indeed, any single male), can experience special stress engendered by the different and often conflicting attitudes toward male-female relationships and roles.

Wives

The problems faced by the American woman abroad are usually many times greater than those faced by her husband.

As limited as the achievements of the women's movement in the United States are, they are still too revolutionary for most of the rest of the world; and the more progress toward liberation the individual American woman has made at home, the more she may find regression from these goals unbearable overseas. And she will become more frustrated if she goes to the overseas assignment thinking that she is going to bring the ideals of the movement to an unenlightened people.

This is true for female college students and single women in other roles, but it is a special dilemma for wives who have accompanied their husbands overseas. The woman who realizes what awaits her and decides to accept her role as housewife and full-time mother has a rich opportunity to learn and grow. But she walks a fine line on the far side of which lie the resentment, frustration, boredom, and depression that are often identified with culture shock. Haggling over prices, managing children who are adjusting to their own unfamiliar and uncomfortable world, discovering different foods (and realizing that many family favorites will no longer be possible to enjoy in the new environment), and surviving the unfamiliar experience of supervising servants for the first time can be gratifying experiences once you've mastered them, but they're often debilitating while in the process.

One of the subtle difficulties to be faced by the American woman living abroad as the spouse of a working husband is the perceived loss of identity she may experience. In many countries foreign spouses are not permitted to work, and the status of women remains rooted in traditional values and behaviors which American women are likely to find objectionable. The struggle to overcome being "the wife-of-so-and-so," rather than a person in her own right, can be a major insult or blow to her self-esteem.

Our best advice: Throw yourself wholeheartedly into exploring the new culture and the new language. Consider the rewards you can get from these new opportunities as a trade-off for the temporary loss of freedom and for the absence of professional opportunities you would be able to pursue back home.

And for the husband, a caution. Don't think that because you are the one who is out there doing the professional work, earning the money, furthering your career, and getting all the recognition, you are somehow engaged in something more important or—and here is where the breakdown most often occurs—more difficult than your wife is. Indeed, the man's involvement in work-related activities actually makes it easier for him to adapt. The husband who brings home sincere understanding and concern for his wife and the problems she is struggling with will help both of them succeed in getting through culture shock to the joys that lie on the other side of the adjustment cycle.

If the wife decides that the sacrifices which the trade-off involves are not worth it, then other arrangements should be considered by the couple. Note also that it is far better to face this issue squarely before the commitment to go overseas is etched in stone.

Single women and the childless spouse who are not students have their own special problems. In many countries outside Western Europe and North America, an unmarried woman living independently is an oddity who will be plied incessantly with questions regarding the whereabouts of her husband, why she isn't married, or whether her father approves of her being there alone. The childless woman will also be subjected continually to the question, "Why don't you have children?" And she will find the answer "I have decided not to have children" utterly incomprehensible to her hosts.

Children

Children who grow up overseas as the offspring of diplomats, military personnel, or missionaries and others whose parents' careers keep them abroad for most or all of their formative years inevitably experience a rootlessness that constitutes a major personal and psychological challenge. This is particularly evident in the difficulty they have in identifying with their homeland (more correctly it should be called the "homeland of their parents"), which, over the years of their youth, they may have visited for only short periods. Many get their first real opportunity to experience the United States when they are sent there to attend college.

Yet studies show that these people—commonly called "third-culture kids"—mature faster, are more independent and introspective, more sophisticated and cosmopolitan, and far more knowledgeable about the world. Perhaps most important, virtually all of them, once they are grown, say they would not trade their international growing-up experience for anything else.

Parents who raise their children, in whole or in part, in another country should get in touch with a very helpful organization named Global Nomads,[1] which is concerned with the special needs of such children as they become adults.

Many aspects of the development of children who spend their formative years growing up in a foreign country are also shared, but to a lesser degree, by children who spend only two or three years abroad. This is especially true of teenagers who, in all likelihood, had to be dragged kicking and screaming onto the plane at the initial departure time. If they are of school age, they will probably find that they have to work harder in the international school than they did in the public school back home. If

---

[1] Global Nomads International, PO Box 9584, Washington, DC 20016, telephone (703) 993-2075.

they attend a local school in their host country, they may find they are expected to do much more memorizing than is done in the States and that discipline is harsher.

American children overseas will also have to be prepared to give up many social pleasures which they are sure they cannot do without—the latest pop music, favorite TV programs, and current movies (though these are increasingly available in countries around the world). Parents will want to help them scout out replacement activities in their new home. They need to be prepared, beforehand, to expect more restrictions on their behavior than they would have at home. Few cultures in the world give children as much freedom as American culture does.

Making new friends and learning the language will be a challenge, and in order to celebrate the traditional holidays their customary way, parents may have to take with them such materials as Easter egg dyes, birthday candles, and sparklers for the Fourth of July.[2]

---

[2] For the reader wishing to explore in greater depth the issues dealt with in this chapter, there are two particularly useful books available: Nancy Piet-Pelon and Barbara Hornby, *Women's Guide to Overseas Living,* 2nd ed. (Yarmouth, ME: Intercultural Press, 1992) and Rosalind Kalb and Penelope Welch, *Moving Your Family Overseas* (Yarmouth, ME: Intercultural Press, 1992).

22

The Challenge

We have called this book a "survival kit" because it deals with the personal pitfalls that await you overseas. We don't, by using the word "survival," envision you at the end of your tour abroad crawling on your hands and knees toward the plane, gaunt, unshaven, clothes in tatters, a hostile landscape behind you. On the contrary, we expect you to survive the overseas experience very much on top.

But it probably won't be easy. Living in a foreign culture is like playing a game you've never played before and for which the rules haven't been explained very well. The challenge is to enjoy the game without missing too many plays and learning the rules and developing skills as you go along.

You'll learn a great deal, though much of it will be intangible and difficult to define. In negotiating the unfamiliar and uncharted territory of another culture, change and growth occur at deep levels, leaving you more competent, more self-assured, and more knowledgeable about yourself and about how the world works.

Bon voyage!

Postscript 1: So You're Coming Back Home?

Why does a book on overseas living have a chapter about coming back home? It's because the traveler needs to consider coming home as part of a complete cycle that includes leaving, settling overseas, and returning.

Just as the success of your overseas experience and your cross-cultural adaptation doesn't need to be left to luck, neither does the success of your return home, though you may reasonably wonder what you could possibly need to do beyond taking care of the bare logistics of the move. You know the language, the ways to get things done and, most likely, you will be returning to family, friends, and a familiar setting. What you may not be aware of is the degree to which you have been changed by the experience and now carry with you a whole new load of cultural baggage. Further, during your absence changes have taken place in the United States—rapid and sometimes radical changes—and reading about them in *Time* or *Newsweek* isn't the same as experiencing them. You may think it will be easy to pick up where you left off; that's where reentry shock comes in.

What Is Reentry Shock?

Some call it reverse culture shock. The culture shock adjustment curve (page 96) is somewhat similar for reentry, though the time frames will probably be different.

You'll recall we said the stages of the adjustment process are:

1. Initial euphoria
2. Irritability and hostility
3. Gradual adjustment, and
4. Adaptation

In Stage 1, you may be very pleased, even euphoric, to be back in your own country, and others may be equally delighted to have you back. But after people express their pleasure at seeing you again and listen politely to your stories for a few minutes, you may suddenly and/or painfully realize that they are not particularly interested in what happened to you abroad and would much prefer to talk about their own affairs. You may also find that the support system you encountered when you first arrived overseas—people who were willing and ready to help you settle into your own community—is not accessible back home. People may help if you ask, but they're busy and you feel embarrassed about being so dependent—especially in your own country!

You may, therefore, find yourself entering Stage 2 more rapidly than you did overseas. Suddenly you are irritated with others and impatient with your own inability to figure out why the way you are doing things doesn't work.

While some people move readily into the adjustment and adaptation stages, others continue to feel alienated, even though they put on the outward appearance of doing well. Underneath, resentment, loneliness, disorientation, and even a sense of helplessness may pervade as they experience the kinds of culture shock symptoms identified in chapter 18. Depression, marital stress, or, in children, regression to earlier stages of development may also be associated with reentry shock.

The gap between you and your family and friends, or your social group at college if you're a student, may be a source of significant irritation. So much that is different will have happened to you and to them that finding common ground will almost certainly be harder than expected.

You also will have learned new things: a foreign language, perhaps, or some local folk dances, or how to bargain in a market. But there's no outlet for them at home. Ways to use your skills can be found, but it takes effort and patience, and the frustrations tend to mount. You may feel let down because daily life in the United States doesn't readily provide the opportunity to meet as many kinds of people as you've known overseas. And the people you do meet seem very provincial and uninterested in things international.

The United States is also different. The politics is shoddier, the pace is more hurried and hectic, there is more violence on TV, and more crime in the streets. In your job you may seem to have less authority, and your work experience abroad may seem irrelevant or at least unappreciated by your colleagues and superiors.

Your status in general is lower, your standard of living goes down. You look like an American but you feel like a stranger. Your spouse feels lonely and out of place—at home! Your children are out of step with their classmates. If you're a college student, your previously selected major may now seem boring, or you may be completely out of sync with your girl- or boyfriend.

In short you will inevitably return from abroad bearing a whole host of expectations which, just as inevitably, will—at least in some degree—be disappointed.

What can you do to counteract reentry shock? In fact, the battle is mostly won when you understand that returning home involves an adjustment process similar to the one you experienced when first going abroad. Indeed, the practical steps we are going to recommend are quite similar to those we suggested for overseas adaptation:

1. Start your exploration of home through sympathetic friends or family members. Share with them some of the *feelings* you have had while living overseas. Sharing feelings instead of experiences sounds less like bragging.

2. Find informants about the United States just as you did about your overseas country. Be the learner. Ask questions about current issues: the price of common products and services, popular entertainment, politics and U.S. foreign policy, the effect of recent changes on the society.

   In other words, play the foreigner. You really *are* in some ways. Learn your "new" culture just as you did your foreign culture. Don't let your new attitudes, values, and *perceptions* (see chapter 17) block that learning process.

3. Ask a friend to make a list of new terms and fads to help you figure out what the current trends are. For instance:

New Vocabulary: (Generation X, cyber-anything, surfing the net, grunge, CDs)

New Technology: (CD-ROMs, digital television, virtual reality, cellular phones, the Internet)

New Foods: (microbreweries, macrobiotic food, low-fat and no-fat food, cappuccino)

What's "in": (in-line skating, snowboarding, body piercing, mountain bikes, sport utility vehicles, luxury cars, banded collar shirts)

What's "out": (tattoos, 10-speed bicycles, economy cars, roller skates, muscle cars)

These examples may seem old by the time you read this, but new ones will replace them.

4. Research various groups that may interest you: churches, clubs, student or professional organizations, international and intercultural groups.

5. Explore places where you might find others with international experience, or seek foreign nationals with whom you can speak the language you've learned and continue to share common experiences you've enjoyed. (Most large and many small colleges and universities have foreign students and scholars on campus, along with active international programs.) You may want to become a host to an exchange student.

Sometimes we get trapped by our emotional responses and misjudge situations and the people around us. When a situation makes you feel uncomfortable, this simple three-step formula may help you deal with it:

First, *describe* (if only to yourself) the situation—what actually do you see happening?

Then *interpret* what you see—what do you think about the situation? What does it mean, objectively?

Finally, *evaluate* the situation—how do you feel about what has taken place?

For example, let's say you have been invited to dinner by an American friend to celebrate your return. You're offered a well-prepared meal consisting of two courses: meat with vegetables and salad followed by dessert. But you have just come from a country where guests are treated with special and elaborate hospitality and are routinely offered a three- or four-course meal (and salad is never served with hot dishes!). You may find this meal disappointing.

1. *Describe:* This is a two-course meal and the food is good.

2. *Interpret:* This is a customary American meal served to guests and among friends and is not an expression of disdain for a guest.

3. *Evaluate:* I feel a little insulted (it doesn't seem special enough for the occasion) but when I get used to this custom, I probably won't react this way.

Now let's try it again with another scenario. You receive a phone call in the office from someone who knows you and hasn't seen you in a few weeks. He identifies himself and immediately makes a request. You have just come from a country where pleasantries are always exchanged before transacting business. It's really difficult for you to launch into a business discussion without first engaging in some social conversation. Using the describe/ interpret/evaluate system, you may come up with something like this:

1. *Describe:* This person is calling for specific information.

2. *Interpret:* The purpose of this call is business and Americans tend to limit their social interaction during working hours.

3. *Evaluate:* I would rather reestablish personal contact before discussing business so that I won't feel simply like an object in the transaction, but since the caller's style doesn't imply a lack of regard for me as a person, I will try to readapt to this American style.

Or, to put it in the context of our earlier discussion of cultural differences, these Americans have some peculiar customs, but they fit together in a logical pattern and are not intended to be offensive. Feelings of disillusion with their own culture sometimes afflict returnees. But take heart, American culture is just different, not wrong!

Postscript 2:
Jaunts and Junkets

Although the principal audience for this survival kit is the American who is going to spend a substantial amount of time living in a country other than the United States, we don't want to ignore entirely the short-term visitor—perhaps a tourist on vacation, a young person exploring another part of the world, or a professional or business executive on a brief assignment abroad. There are many things such a person can do—before, during, and after the trip—to insure getting the maximum return from the experience.

Predeparture Preparations

1. *Check both national and local holidays.* Especially if your stay is short, you don't want to be immobilized because everything is shut down. Holidays may be specific to a city or region as well as national. In Catholic countries (such as Italy, Spain, and Latin American countries), for instance, many cities cel-

ebrate their patron saint's day by shutting down businesses for several days. On the other hand, you may actually *want* to time your visit to coincide with an especially colorful, unique, or interesting holiday.

2. *Check linguistic variations within the country.* In China, for example, while Mandarin is the official language, there are ten major regional dialects and minor linguistic variations. The differences in the major languages are as great as between European languages. There may also be tensions within the country over language use. In Spain for instance, speakers of Catalán in and around Barcelona are proud of their linguistic heritage. Using even a smattering of Catalán (especially if you are able and intend to speak Spanish) will make a favorable impression.

3. *Research special customs or cultural traits* of the region you are going to. Nothing will have a greater payoff among the nationals of that region than evidence, through some comment or other, that you realize how special the people there are.

4. *Read at least one general history of the country* (or at least the history section of a good travel guide).

5. *Check out the current political situation and economic conditions,* especially as they might relate to the United States.

6. *Line up your contacts,* personal or business, well ahead of time before leaving the States.

   If you do not receive confirmation of appointments before you leave, try when you are there to make contact anyway. There are many reasons—technical and intercultural—why people fail to respond to appointment requests from abroad.

Even if there are no logical contacts (those directly related to your business, professional, or personal purposes for traveling abroad) for you to arrange ahead of time, you might want to try the Internet. Just making one special contact is worth the effort, since it may be an opening to others.

Once you have arrived, the commercial attaché of the American embassy or consulate may be willing to arrange appointments for you. If you want more than one or two, contact the attaché before departing from the United States. If the purpose of your visit merits it, it may be possible for you to receive special briefings from the political and economic officers at the American embassy as well.

7. *Take gifts.* It is not easy to find small gifts which cannot also be purchased around the world these days. The time when people everywhere were thrilled to receive a disposable ballpoint pen from an American visitor is long gone, but with a little ingenuity you will be able to come up with some good ideas. Here are a few suggestions: something with your company's or university's logo or some other special emblem on it; coffee-table books focusing on the United States, your city, or perhaps your host's special interests; cassette recordings or CDs that fit the tastes of the recipients; books, for people who speak English, on American slang or American idioms. Artifacts made by Native Americans are par-

ticularly appreciated and unavailable in most foreign countries.

Larger gifts, perhaps for homestays or for someone who has done you a big favor, might include a small Navajo rug or a patchwork quilt. Two of the things which even European visitors (who can buy practically anything at home) appreciate from the United States are top-quality Turkish towels and percale sheets. One unusually ingenious friend took the gift I wish I had thought of: an uncut sheet of dollar bills (which can be purchased directly from the U.S. Treasury Department in Washington, D.C.).

8. *Attend to logistics.* Consult your travel agent about ground transportation from the airport at your destination to your hotel before you leave the States. This information is very helpful to know in advance, especially if your trip entails stopovers in several cities. Don't forget that American Express in practically every major city in the world can, for a price, provide such special services as meeting you at the airport with prearranged transportation, local city guides and guided tour arrangements, interpreters (if needed), etc.

Know where your hotels are located. Avoid the surprise upon arrival of finding the hotel you've chosen (perhaps because it was cheaper) is also outside the city, a long way from most of your appointments or places you wanted to see.

Err on the side of clothing that is more, rather than less, formal.

In-Country

1. Communication

Even in countries where the lingua franca is English, watch out for communication problems. Don't automatically assume that everything you say will be understood as you intended it. Check, verify, and paraphrase in order to see that what you meant is what was actually understood by the other party. In a foreign culture, it often takes twice the time and effort to communicate effectively.

Small talk can be especially difficult for the short-term visitor. It may surprise you to learn that in some countries it is inappropriate to ask your host "Are you married?" or "Do you have any children?" Such questions are all considered—in France, for instance—far too personal to ask someone you are meeting for the first time. (In other countries, e.g., those of the Arab world, these kinds of questions are the most appropriate!) Some research on small-talk customs in the countries you are visiting is needed. It may interest you to know that in many parts of the world questions that are taboo in the United States—like "How old are you?" "How much do you weigh?" "What price did you pay for your suit/your car/your home?" or "What is your salary?"—are not taboo at all.

Even on a short visit you should attempt to make some penetrating observations of your host country. One way is to go armed with one or two (no more) questions that, from your predeparture research, you have identified as significant to the country and of interest to you personally (though not too politically charged). Then ask everyone you meet in that country the same one or two questions. The insights you get from this brief and simple polling exercise will be striking and will provide you with the ability to make some remarkably cogent observations on your return home.

2. Scout

A helpful device to process experiences and information gathered during your time abroad is a procedure known by the acronym **SCOUT**.[1]

It is a five-step process:

One: *Suspend judgment.*

Suspend judgment in your interactions with your hosts. Otherwise, you will be passing judgment according to cultural assumptions you are familiar with—most likely those of mainstream American culture—but which simply do not apply in the foreign culture as they do at home.

Two: *Collect data.*

Gather information about events that occur which you don't feel you understand. Check the context and look for details you might have missed.

Three: *Organize information.*

What are all the possible alternative explanations and interpretations of your data?

Four: *Utilize resources.*

Tap into your network of contacts for help in reading the situation in the context of the new culture, that is, ask for advice from people who understand the culture.

Five: *Test results.*

Evaluate the data you obtained from the prior four steps, come up with an explanation, then test your thesis in future similar situations. Correct any misjudgments as you gather new information and make new, more accurate interpretations.

---

[1] Created and copyrighted by Claude Schnier of Global Vision Group, Oakland, California.

3. Customs

Invitations. Look for differences in the way dinner or other social invitations are extended and get advice on the social protocol in your host country.

The same goes for receiving invitations, though we suggest one general principle: accept. Socializing with colleagues is typically more obligatory in most parts of the world than it is in the United States. Also check, if necessary, whether spouses are included. In some cultures they are not.

Respect for authority. Few countries are as egalitarian in social conduct as the United States. How do you respond in cultures where one is expected to demonstrate more respect and deference than you are used to demonstrating to those who hold positions of authority? The best approach is simply to watch how other people do it.

Formality and informality. The casual style of Americans often offends people in other countries without our being aware of it. The alternative style, being diplomatic rather than bluntly direct, unfortunately does not come naturally to most Americans. Abroad, it helps to moderate our directness with a little sensitive indirection.

Time. In many parts of the world, time is a different commodity from what North Americans perceive it to be. Being an hour late for an appointment may not be considered late, or the person with whom you have an appointment may cancel at the last minute without considering it rude. These are different kinds of cultural behaviors, not attempts to insult you. The best response: Cultivate your patience, and be prepared to fill the time productively.

Follow-Up

After returning home (or on the way), spend a little time cataloging what you've discovered about the country or countries you visited. You will probably be surprised at the insights you generate in this kind of after-the-fact diary and how useful it will be in conversations with friends and colleagues or in reports to your supervisors. Use the data gleaned from the informal poll recommended earlier.

Write or phone (as seems to be preferred in most Latin countries) key people you met on your trip. Send prints of the snapshots you took of them.

Finally, in the months after returning home, reading a few novels set in the country or countries you visited will fuel the interest started by your trip abroad. *Traveler's Reading Guides* by Maggy Simony (see Appendix E) include several excellent novels which take place in the world's countries, and your local librarian will probably be able to recommend more.

Appendix A

The Kluckhohn Model

ORIENTATION	RANGE					
	Basically Evil		Neutral	Mixture of Good and Evil	Basically Good	
	Mutable	Immutable	Mutable	Immutable	Mutable	Immutable
Human Nature						
Relationship to Nature	Subjugation to Nature		Harmony with Nature		Mastery over Nature	
Sense of Time	Past-oriented (Tradition-bound)		Present-oriented (Situational)		Future-oriented (Goal-oriented)	
Activity	Being (Expressive/Emotional)		Being-in-Becoming* (Inner Development)		Doing (Action-oriented)	
Social Relationships	Lineality** (Authoritarian)		Collaterality*** (Collective Decisions)		Individualism**** (Equal Rights)	

Explanations of Terms Used Above

*Being-in-Becoming—The personality is given to containment and control by means of such activities as meditation and detachment, for the purpose of the development of the self as a unified whole.

**Lineality—Lines of authority clearly established and dominant-subordinate relationships clearly defined and respected.

***Collaterality—A human being is an individual and also a member of many groups and subgroups; he/she is independent and dependent.

****Individualism—Autonomy of the individual.

Source: Florence Kluckhohn and Frederick Strodtbeck, *Variations in Value Orientations* (Evanston: IL: Row, Peterson, 1961). (See especially chapter 1.)

In terms of the *values* they represent, the Kluckhohn Model would look like this:

ORIENTATION	RANGE		
Human Nature	Most people can't be trusted.	There are both evil people and good people in the world, and you have to check people out to find out which they are.	Most people are basically pretty good at heart.
Relationship to Nature	Life is largely determined by external forces, such as God, fate, or genetics. A person can't surpass the conditions life has set.	Humans should, in every way, live in complete harmony with nature.	Humans' challenge is to conquer and control nature. Everything from air conditioning to the "green revolution" has resulted from having met this challenge.
Sense of Time	Humans should learn from history and attempt to emulate the glorious ages of the past.	The present moment is everything. Let's make the most of it. Don't worry about tomorrow, enjoy today.	Planning and goal setting make it possible to accomplish miracles. A little sacrifice today will bring a better tomorrow.
Activity	It's enough to just "be." It's not necessary to accomplish great things in life to feel your life has been worthwhile.	Humans' main purpose for being placed on this earth is for their own inner development.	If people work hard and apply themselves fully, their efforts will be rewarded.
Social Relationships	Some people are born to lead others. There are leaders and there are followers.	Whenever I have a serious problem, I like to get the advice of my family or close friends on how best to solve it.	All people should have equal rights and complete control over their own destiny.

Appendix B

Information-Gathering Checklist about Your Host Country

The following is a guide to help you gather basic facts about the country you are going to. It is not essential that you follow the exact sequence given here. If you're especially interested in Section F, for example, start there.

A. Symbols

Symbolism of flag

National anthem

Myths and legends of ethnic group(s)

National flower, etc.

National holidays

Traditional dress

B. Human and natural resources

Geography and topography

Regional characteristics

Major cities

Natural resources (flora, fauna, minerals)

Climate

Demographic information

Transportation system

Communications system

Mass communication media

C. Family and social structure

Family life

Role differentiation among family members

Social classes

Male/female relationships

Friendships

Social organizations

Social welfare

Customs (re: birth, marriage, death, etc.) and courtesies

D. Religion and philosophy

Religious beliefs (indigenous and borrowed)

Philosophy (Cartesian, inductive, pragmatic, collectivist, individualistic, fatalistic)

Proverbs

Superstitions

E. Education

General approach (e.g., rote memorization vs. problem-solving approach)

School system

Colleges and universities

Vocational training

F. Fine arts and cultural achievements

Painting

Sculpture

Crafts

Folk arts

Architecture

Music

Dance

Drama

Literature

Poetry

Cinema

G. Economics and industry

Principal industries

Exports/imports

Foreign investment

Cottage industries (if any)

Industrial development

Modernization (if applicable)

Urban and rural conditions

Agriculture (crops and animal husbandry)

Fishing (if it is a major activity)

Marketing systems

Money

H. Politics and Government

System of government

Political parties

Government organization (national and local)

Current political figures

Police system

Military

I. Science

Inventions and achievements

Medicine

Research

J. Sports and games

Sports unique to the country

Modern world sports

Traditional children's games

K. Foods

Dietary restrictions

Unique products

Special cooking techniques

L. Language

Local dialects/ languages

Appendix C

A Human Profile

Questions about social processes, values, and behaviors for the Grandparent Exercise

What would you teach your grandchildren about:

- Whom they should obey?
- How many children they should have?
- Who makes decisions (at home, in school, in the community)?
- What is expected of children when they are young? And after their parents get old?
- How to behave with others (public officials, family members, neighbors, old people, other children, salespeople, etc.)?
- What to depend upon others for?
- When to be self-sufficient?
- Whom to respect and how to show respect for others?
- What they can expose to others and what should be kept private or secret?
- How they should act in public so they will be a credit to or bring honor upon the family?

- How to plan for the future?
- What should be remembered from their heritage?
- How important they are and can expect to be in the community?
- What was better when you were young?
- Whom they should seek advice from when they need it?
- What you wish for your grandchildren that you could not be or have?
- Whom to trust?
- What it means to be successful in life?
- What it is they can depend upon as always being good or important?
- What the signs of success are?
- What provides "security"?
- Why people work?
- What they should be wary or afraid of?
- What type of work they should prepare to do?
- How they can improve on what they are or have?
- Who their friends should be?
- Where they should live?
- What things in nature are beautiful?
- Whom they should marry and at what age?
- What they should be willing to sacrifice to insure a better life for more people?

Appendix D

Checklists of Logistics

The following lists are suggestive rather than exhaustive. You will probably add items which fit the particular country you are entering.

Preparations for Assignment Abroad

Official documents

Apply for passport and any necessary visas. It is advisable to have separate passports for each family member. If the children are on the mother's passport, neither mother nor children can travel outside the country independently.

Doctors

Make appointments for medical examinations for each family member well in advance, three months ahead if possible, in order to be finished with any needed series immunizations a month before departure date.

Request copies of important records, X rays, or prescriptions to go with you. Have prescriptions written in generic terms rather than with brand names.

Be sure to have each person's blood type in case a transfusion is needed.

Inquire about gamma globulin shots as a preventive measure against hepatitis.

Arrange to have copies of eyeglass prescriptions for any member of the family using glasses, as well as an extra pair of glasses for each.

Make dental appointments for each family member well in advance so all needed work can be completed by your dentist. Request instructions on fluoride treatment abroad for children. Ask for copies of records, X rays, and a statement of any recommended orthodontic treatment.

See your veterinarian for required shots and certificates if you are taking a pet with you. Write ahead to the United States embassy in your country for current information on pet entry requirements, especially quarantine regulations. Consult with your veterinarian about preferred travel arrangements for your pet. Determine whether it will be necessary to inform someone abroad if the pet is to arrive in advance of the family.

Lawyer

Each adult member of the family should have an up-to-date will, properly witnessed and signed with the original placed in a safety deposit box, a copy for your lawyer, and a copy in your possession.

Draw up a power of attorney and leave it with a responsible relative or friend so that you have someone who can act legally in your behalf while you are abroad.

Bank

Arrange with your home bank to mail your monthly statements to you via airmail. Original naturalization papers can never be replaced, so it is best to travel with copies only of these documents. Arrange power of attorney for someone within easy traveling distance of your bank to have access to your safety deposit box. The bank will need to register authorization and signature.

Obtain a supply of local currency for those countries to which you will be traveling to cover porters' tips, taxi fares, etc.

Purchase traveler's checks (preferably in small denominations) to cover hotel, restaurant, and sightseeing expenses while en route.

Put credit cards in safety deposit box until your return, except for credit cards you expect to use while abroad.

Schools

Notify your children's teachers of departure date in case special examinations must be scheduled to allow completion of term work. Obtain grade reports, test results, teacher evaluations, samples of work, etc. to facilitate placement in the new school.

Write schools in the new city for information or, if you are able to make a school selection prior to arrival, notify the school of your children's anticipated date of arrival, indicate their grade level, and request that space be held for them.

Insurance

Arrange for adequate personal liability insurance (to cover injuries to people on your property while you are gone) and insurance to cover your household effects and luggage. Marine insurance for automobiles should be specific. If keeping your automobile insurance from the United States, check to see if it covers your country of assignment. Some insurance companies abroad will give reduced rates if you produce a letter from your own company showing an accident-free record.

Ascertain that you have appropriate health insurance coverage for yourself and your family.

Post office

Complete a change of address card for your local post office. Obtain a supply of these to send to the Internal Revenue Service, Department of Motor Vehicles, magazine subscriptions, etc.

Notify all charge accounts and cancel magazine and newspaper subscriptions or change to your new address.

Provide your family and friends with specific information on how to mail letters and packages to you. In some countries the duty will exceed the value of the package, so you may want to warn against sending gifts. (This information may be hard to obtain before you arrive overseas.)

Check absentee voting procedure in case any special registration is required.

Obtain an international driver's license through the American Automobile Association (AAA).

Give notice of your moving date to all utility companies—gas, oil, water, electricity, telephone, etc., and discuss arrangements for billing and/or discontinuing service. Also notify any other delivery service you may use, such as Federal Express or UPS.

Keep records of official expenses involved in the move.

Important Papers to Accompany You

On your person:

1. Passport
2. Shot records

3. Internationally recognized credit cards
4. U.S. and international driver's licenses (plan to renew U.S. license by mail, if possible)

In your briefcase:
1. Copies of insurance policies
2. School records
3. Medical and dental records
4. Power of attorney
5. Will
6. Inventories of personal luggage, air freight, and household shipments
7. Extra passport photos
8. Record of your car's serial number

Embassy Information

Consular officials and their duties

The chief of mission with the title of ambassador, minister, or chargé d'affaires, and the deputy chief of mission are the heads of diplomatic missions. They are responsible for all parts of the mission within a country, including the consular post or posts.

The economic/commercial officers represent all the commercial interests in the country to which they are assigned. Their responsibilities include the promotion of trade and exports, arranging appointments for their citizens with local businesspeople and government officials, and providing the maximum possible assistance to their country's businesses within the host country.

Political officers study and report on local political developments and their possible effects on their country's interests.

Labor officers are well informed on labor in their particular countries and can supply information on wages, nonwage costs, local security regulations, etc.

The consular officers are the ones with whom you, as an expatriate, will have the most contact. Their function is to give you and your property the protection of your government.

They maintain lists of their citizens living in the area, have lists of local attorneys, and act as liaison with police and other officials.

The administrative officer is in charge of the normal business operations of the post, including all purchasing for the embassy or consulate.

When you first arrive in your host country, register with the embassy or consulate nearest you. If there is an emergency, your relatives and friends will be able to locate you easily.

In addition, it will be useful to inquire about:

Weather/climate conditions: What fabrics wear longer, what special care personal and household items require?

Postal system: Dependability and efficiency of the postal system, location and appearance of post boxes, cost of mailing letters and packages.

Clothing sizes and availability: What will have to be carried with you, what clothing sizes translate into a size 12 dress or 9 shoe, the advisability of having clothes tailored?

Electricity: What voltage is used in the host country, can your appliances (including hair dryers) be adapted, which appliances are best left at home?

Housing: Can arrangements be made prior to arrival; if not, where will you stay temporarily, how do you search for housing, what agreements with landlords are customary?

Furnishings and appliances: What "travels" well, how much shipping weight will you be allowed, when can shipped household items be expected to arrive, what is supplied in your new home (if you have acquired one)?

Servants: Are servants available, how many will you need, how are they engaged, what are the customary wages, benefits, and obligations of employers, what bonuses or special gifts are given, how are unsatisfactory servants dismissed?

Food restrictions (if any): What foods are unavailable, what are appropriate substitutes, what items will you want to import?

Health and hospitals: Where do you get emergency and other health care in-country?

Schools: Can your children attend public schools, what alternative schools are available, what are registration procedures, will uniforms be needed, is it necessary to place children in boarding schools at home or in a nearby country?

Shopping: Who does the shopping, how often does one shop for food, what kinds of stores for food and other necessities are available?

Babysitting arrangements: Who babysits, how is a sitter hired, what are the customary rates, are sitters picked up and returned home?

Laws and legal systems: What are the traffic laws, driving customs and conditions, obligations in case of an accident? We trust that you will not encounter the law in other instances but it is useful to know if there are any *unfamiliar* laws that you might break, literally by accident. For example, is it illegal to have liquor in your possession?

Employment possibilities for spouses: In most countries it is illegal to work without official permission. In many cases those who accompany a spouse employed by a foreign firm are not permitted to work.

Appendix E

Resources for Further Information

African American Institute publishes one-page summary sheets of each African country (periodically updated). African American Institute, 833
United Nations Plaza, New York, NY 10017.

Background Notes contain a few pages of demographic data, geographic and historical over-
views, travel tips, and a brief summary of
American relations with over 180 countries.
Distributed by the Superintendent of Documents, U.S. Government Printing Office, Washington, DC 20402, for a minimal cost.

Bibliographic Surveys are annotated bibliographies
prepared by the Department of the Army for
certain areas of the world. Such volumes are
available from the Superintendent of Documents, U.S. Government Printing Office, Washington, DC 20402.

Business Customs & Protocol series, produced for
businesspeople, concentrate on how to get
started, how to get things done, and how to
facilitate mutual understanding. Produced by
and available from Stanford Research Institute

International, 333 Ravenswood Ave., Menlo Park, CA 94025.

Cities of the World is a publication on more than 140 countries of the world, covering over 2,000 major and minor cities in Africa, Europe, the Americas, Asia, and Australia. Gale Research, Book Tower, Detroit, MI 48226.

Country Studies have superseded the former *Area Handbooks.* Each volume of the series covers a specific country. These provide detailed geographical, historical, ethnological, and political data. Published by the Federal Research Division of the U.S. Library of Congress. Available from the Superintendent of Documents, Washington, DC 20402.

Cultural Atlas series capture the immense diversity and richness of the countries they cover. Available from Facts on File, 460 Park Ave. South, New York, NY 10016.

Culture Shock! [specific country] is a series of publications with general as well as specific tips on cultural adjustment to the country and its customs. Available in most U.S. bookstores or, for a complete catalogue, write Graphic Arts Center Publishing, PO Box 10306, Portland, OR 97210.

Do's and Taboos around the World: A Guide to International Behavior (edited by Roger Axtell) gives a limited and uneven but nonetheless useful coverage of protocol, jargon, customs, and etiquette for more than 90 countries. Compiled by the Parker Pen Co. and available from John Wiley, 605 Third Ave., New York, NY 10158. Also available from Audio Forum.

Economist Intelligence Publications provide a variety of materials, including the *Quarterly Economic Review*, covering more than 150 countries; special *Intelligence Unit Reports*; *Quarterly Energy Review*; and much more. Available from The Economist Intelligence Unit, 75 Rockefeller Plaza, New York, NY 10019.

Encyclopedia Britannica provides extensive demographic, historical, geographic, and social country and area data. Current demographic data and significant political events are provided in the *Britannica Book of the Year*. Encyclopedia Britannica, 3105 Michigan Ave., Chicago, IL 60604.

The Encyclopedia of Peoples of the World contains more than 2,000 alphabetical entries on all peoples and ethnic groups of the world. Published by Henry Holt, 4375 W. 1980 South, Salt Lake City, UT 84104.

The Encyclopedia of the Third World by George T. Kurian is published by Facts on File, 460 Park Ave. South, New York, NY 10016. There are three volumes in the series, sold only as a set, so you will probably want to check a library for this one.

The Europa World Yearbook, two volumes, published by Europa, Ltd. of London and distributed by Gale Research, Book Tower, Detroit, MI 48226. This is an excellent source for listings of international organizations. Europa, Ltd. also publishes other regional titles in their Regional surveys of the World series including: *Middle East and North Africa; Far East and Australasia; Africa South of the Sahara; and South America, Central America and the Caribbean.*

Health Information for International Travel is an annual publication that includes helpful information for travelers. Available from the Department of Health and Human Services, Public Health Service, Centers for Disease Control and Prevention, Atlanta, GA 30333.

Human Relations Area Files/The Outlines of World Cultures indexes, on microfiche, cover every area of the world from an anthropological perspective. Detailed information is presented on many of the ethnic groups of each country. Available at major university libraries throughout the United States. Human Relations Area Files, 755 Prospect St., New Haven, CT 06511.

InterAct series. Available for Eastern Europe, the Arab world, and ten individual countries: Australia, China, Greece, Israel, Japan, Mexico, the Philippines, Russia, Spain, and Thailand (more volumes in press; inquire for complete current list). Synthesize cross-cultural conflict analysis, ethnic personality characteristics, social relationships, sex roles, family and communication styles, and attitudes. Format compares and contrasts the specific country with the United States. Published by Intercultural Press, PO Box 700, Yarmouth, ME 04096.

International Business Traveler's Companion, Donald E. deKeiffer. The ultimate guide and sourcebook for the international business traveler. Intercultural Press, PO Box 700, Yarmouth, ME 04096.

(Craighead's) International Executive Travel and Relocation Service provides essential, up-to-date information for people on overseas assignments. International Executive Update Service, PO Box 149, Darien, CT 06820.

Internet, a global interconnection of computer networks, allows users worldwide to exchange electronic mail nearly instantaneously; to read "bulletin boards" on many topics, including world cultures; and to access an unlimited repository of government, commercial, and privately compiled information in any area of interest.

Lands & Peoples, published by Grolier in six volumes, covers history, geography, sociology, anthropology, economics, and the political situation in each of the countries covered. Grolier, Sherman Turnpike, Danbury, CT 06816.

Managing Cultural Differences by Phillip R. Harris and Robert T. Moran details strategies for managers and specific area guidelines and resources. Gulf Publishing, PO Box 2608, Houston, TX 77252.

Moving Your Family Overseas. Designed for use by the entire family, this book discusses the challenges of moving abroad faced by each member of the family. Available from Intercultural Press, PO Box 700, Yarmouth, ME 04096.

The Nations around Us. Volume 1 includes CulturGrams (4-page briefings) on 50 nations of North and South America and Western and Eastern Europe. Volume 2 covers 39 countries of the Middle East, Africa, Asia, and the Pacific. Each contains information about such things as customary greetings, conversational styles, gestures and their meanings, customs and background of the population, land, economy, religion, history, climate, and government. CulturGrams are also available individually. Available from Garrett Park Press, PO Box 190B, Garrett Park, MD 20896.

Political Handbook of the World, edited by Arthur S. Banks, has up-to-date information about every independent country in the world. CSA Publications, Center for Social Analysis, SUNY at Binghamton, Binghamton, NY 13902.

The Reader's Guide to Periodical Literature allows one to search recent magazines and periodicals for pertinent articles on each country. Available in most libraries.

A Selected Functional and Country Bibliography for [specific country] is the basic title for excellent bibliographies on eight major geographic areas of the world. They are updated regularly and are useful for creating you own up-to-date bibliography. Available from the Center for Area and Community Studies, National Foreign Affairs Training Center, 4000 Arlington Blvd., Arlington, VA 22204.

Snowdon's Global Protocols: The Americas and *Snowdon's Official International Protocols.* The latter has three volumes—Asia-Pacific Rim, Europe, and the Definitive Guide to Business and Social Customs of the World. Irwin Professional Publishing, 1333 Burr Ridge Pkwy., Burr Ridge, IL 60521.

Statesman's Year-Book provides background information on every country in the world, including brief histories and explanations of government and monetary systems.

The World Today series consist of six volumes covering Africa, Latin America, the Middle East and South Asia, the Far East and the Southwest Pacific, the (former) Soviet Union and Eastern Europe, and Europe. You may purchase them from Stryker-Post Publications, 888 17th St., NW, Washington, DC 20006.

Third World Economic Handbook by Stuart Sinclair provides country surveys of more than 20 major Third World countries with emphasis on their economies and state of development. Published by Euromonitor Publications, Ltd., London. Available from Gale Research, Book Tower, Detroit, MI 48226.

Traveler's Reading Guides: Ready-made Reading Lists for the Armchair Traveler, edited by Maggy Simony, provide bibliographies for the world's countries in three volumes. Volume 1 covers Europe, Vol. II, the Americas, and Vol. III, the rest of the world. References include fiction set in the countries listed as well as significant articles from past issues of *National Geographic.* Facts on File, 460 Park Ave. South, New York, NY 10016.

Islam: Understanding your sponsored child's religion is one in a series of brochures designed to help Plan International participants better understand and communicate with children they sponsor in those regions of the world. Others in the series include *Hinduism, Buddhism,* and *Christianity.* Childreach (U.S. member Plan International), 155 Plan Way, Warwick, RI 02886.

WeEuropeans by Richard Hill offers a qualitative and objective assessment of the different temperaments present in the European community. Available from Intercultural Press, PO Box 700, Yarmouth, ME 04096.

Whole World Guide to Culture Learning by Dan Hess. A text for culture learning which offers a substantive introduction to the ideas which provide the framework for culture learning along with extensive practical guidelines on how to extract the desired learning from the cross-cultural experience. Intercultural Press, PO Box 700, Yarmouth, ME 04096.

Women's Guide to Overseas Living by Nancy Piet-Pelon and Barbara Hornby is a sensitive examination of issues critical to women and families who go abroad to live. Available from Intercultural Press, PO Box 700, Yarmouth, ME 04096.

World Cultures Database (published on diskettes in journal installments) is a working tool for cross-cultural research and instruction. Published by World Cultures, PO Box 12524, La Jolla, CA 92037.

The World Factbook contains brief fact sheets with demographic data. Updated annually. Central Intelligence Agency, Washington, DC 20505.

The World in Figures (published annually) provides statistical and marketing information on each country. Featured are population figures, national income, standard of living, main commodities, world trade, inflation rates, currency, plus political and economic summaries and much more. Published by the *Economist*, available through Rand McNally & Co., PO Box 7600, Chicago, IL 60680.

World Weather Guide is a country-by-country guide to the average temperature and climatic conditions at any time of the year. New York Times Books, 229 W. 43rd St., New York, NY 10036.

Many classic studies of specific peoples of the world are found in major libraries. A few representative titles include:

Among the Believers: An Islamic Journey by V. S. Naipaul (covers Iran, Pakistan, Malaysia, and Indonesia).

The Arab Mind, by Raphael Patai.

The Chrysanthemum and the Sword (Japan), by Ruth Benedict.

The French, by Theodore Zeldin.

The Germans, by Gordon Craig.

The Italians, by Luigi Barzini.

The Japanese Mind, by Charles Moore.

Korean Patterns, by Paul Crane.

The Russians and *The New Russians*, by Hedrick Smith.

The Ways of Thinking of Eastern Peoples (India, China, Tibet, and Japan), by Hajime Nakamura.

(See InterAct series for more.)

Travel Publications

Names of some of the more widely used travel guides series are: AAA, Access Guide, All the Best, American Express, A to Z (by Robert Kane), Bazak, Baedeker, Benn, Berlitz, Birnbaum, Eye Witness, Fielding, Fodor (which now includes People Briefings section, which is excellent), Ford, Frommer, Handbook Series, Insight, Knopf Guides, Let's Go, Lonely Planet, McKay, Michelin, Moon, Myra Waldo, Nagel, New Horizons, Olson, Pan Am, Phaidan, Putnam, and Rand McNally.

The Travel Book: Guide to the Travel Guides (by John O. Heise and Julia Rinehart) is an index with short descriptions of the travel guides on the market. A second part of the book suggests which travel guide should be used for each country. Scarecrow Press, 52 Liberty St., Metuchen, NJ 08840.

The Traveller's Bookstore stocks travel books plus histories and novels on many countries. Traveller's Bookstore, 22 West 52nd St., New York, NY 10019.

Weissmann Travel Reports will provide a current report on any single country in the world. These reports are especially useful for the less accessible countries (like North Korea or Laos, or the former Soviet Central Asian republics) for which information is particularly difficult to get. Data is updated four times per year, so it is reliable. Weissmann Travel Reports, Box 49279, Austin, TX 78765.

Films and Videos

Films and videos are often difficult to locate because few master sources reference all the films available for any particular country. Selections often must be made from the brief description given in a listing rather than through viewing the film or video.

The Educational Film Locator of the Consortium of University Film Centers is unquestionably the best single source for identifying films on any subject, including countries and areas. Although it lists large numbers of films by title for each country (well over 200 for Japan, for example) and where each is available, its single shortcoming is the failure to give annotated descriptions of the films. The publisher is R. R. Bowker, 245 West 17th St., New York, NY 10011. This source is available in major libraries; be sure to locate the latest edition.

Crossing Cultures through Film by Ellen Summerfield. Describes over 70 classic films in detail including how to make most effective use of them in classroom and training situations. Available from Intercultural Press, PO Box 700, Yarmouth, ME 04096.

Film and Video Resources for International Educational Exchange by Lee Ziegler. Provides brief annotations on 250 films and videos. Published by NAFSA: Association of International Educators and available from Intercultural Press, PO Box 700, Yarmouth, ME 04096.

The latest edition of the *Video Source Book* is up to date, but there is less available commercially on video than there is on film. The most useful section in locating country-specific videos is titled "Subject Category Index." Published by the National Video Clearinghouse, 100 Lafayette Dr., Syosset, NY 11791.

Since more country and regional videos are released all the time, be sure to check with local video rental outlets as well as local library branches.

Additional Services

The embassies and consulates of the world's nations are generally willing to provide informative materials and respond to specific questions. However, the usefulness of the publications and the level of responsiveness to inquiries varies greatly. This is often due to the financial resources available for any given country. Japan, Germany, and Saudi Arabia are particularly known for the extensive publications they produce. The more specific you can be in your request, the more likely you are to get what you need. Many countries also operate special tourist offices which concentrate on attracting tourists to their countries. Colorful booklets and attractive posters are available from many of them. Up-to-date addresses for all these embassies, consulates, tourist-trade offices, etc., can be located in major public or university libraries. For example, check the *Federal Staff Directory* (published annually), Congressional Staff Directory Ltd., Mt. Vernon, VA 22121.

Maps

Excellent editions of maps are available for all areas and countries, and most cities of the world. Allow time for ordering.

American Map Co., H6-35 57th Rd., Maspeth, NY 11378, is a well-stocked map store.

Atlas of the World Today, edited by Neil Grand and Nick Middleton, provides a world picture in political and social framework maps. Harper Collins, 10 E. 53rd St., New York, NY 10022.

The Central Intelligence Agency publishes many unclassified maps, making them available to the general public for purchase through the Government Printing Office in Washington, DC. (Be aware that the GPO may take several months to fill mail orders, so allow plenty of time.)

Defense Mapping Agency (formerly known as the Army Map Service), 6101 McArthur Blvd., Washington, DC 20315, is another government-sponsored source of maps from which anyone may order.

Hagstrom Map and Travel Center, 57 West 43rd St., New York, NY 10036, is an excellent source for maps. In addition, it publishes a free quarterly newsletter full of information on new maps from many publishers.

Library of Congress Map Room will provide information by phone [(202) 278-6277] on where a map for any city in the world may be obtained.

Library of Congress Map Division, James Madison Memorial Bldg., LMB101, Washington, DC 20540.

A. J. Nystrom Co., 3333 Elston Ave., Chicago, IL 60618, is a source for raised relief maps.

Rand McNally Co., 150 East 52nd St., New York, NY 10022, has maps of the world. Branches are located in major U.S. cities.

Travel Centers of the World, PO Box 1788-JA, Hollywood, CA 90078, is perhaps the most complete source of world maps. It offers maps and travel guides of cities and countries. Their 350-page catalogue is expensive, but is well worth the investment.

An extremely useful map resource is *The Map Catalog* (Joel Makower, editor). New York: Vintage Books, 201 E. 50th St., New York, NY 10022. In addition to making you aware of an amazing number of types of maps which are available, it also includes a helpful section on where to find indigenous maps in more than 135 countries around the world.

About the Author

L. Robert Kohls is Senior Research Fellow at the San Francisco-based management consulting firm of Global Vision Group. Kohls spent seven years in the private sector (Westinghouse and Time Inc.) and ten years with the U.S. Foreign Service. Retired in 1992 from the position of Director of the Office of International Programs at San Francisco State University, he has thirty years' experience as an intercultural trainer and trainer of other trainers. With over 130,000 copies in print, *Survival Kit for Overseas Living* is considered a classic in the field. Kohls has lived, worked, and traveled in more than 80 countries with extensive stays in Asia, Africa, the Middle East, Latin America, and Europe. A founding member of SIETAR International, he was, in 1986, the first recipient of the Society's most prestigious award, *Primus inter pares.*